Routledge Revivals

The Origin and Development of the Bengali Language

First published in 1972, *The Origin and Development of the Bengali Language (Vol. 3)* is the updated supplement to the two-volume *The Origin and Development of the Bengali Language.* It contains certain additions and corrections to the first systematic and detailed history of a Modern Indo-Aryan Language written by an Indian, and incidentally, as it is comparative in its treatment, taking into consideration facts in other Indo-Aryan speeches, it is an invaluable contribution to the scientific study of the Modern Indo-Aryan languages as a whole. This book will be of interest to students of language, linguistics and South Asian studies.

The Origin and Development of the Bengali Language

Volume Three

Suniti Kumar Chatterji

Routledge
Taylor & Francis Group
ROUTLEDGE REVIVALS

First published in 1972
By George Allen & Unwin Ltd

This edition first published in 2024 by Routledge
4 Park Square, Milton Park, Abingdon, Oxon, OX14 4RN
and by Routledge
605 Third Avenue, New York, NY 10017

Routledge is an imprint of the Taylor & Francis Group, an informa business

ISBN: 978-1-032-77046-8 (hbk)
ISBN: 978-1-003-48118-8 (ebk)
ISBN: 978-1-032-77068-0 (pbk)

Book DOI 10.4324/9781003481188

THE ORIGIN AND DEVELOPMENT OF THE BENGALI LANGUAGE

BY SUNITI KUMAR CHATTERJI

M.A. (Calcutta), D.Litt. (London)
Emeritus Professor of Comparative Philology in the University of Calcutta
National Professor of India in Humanities

WITH A FOREWORD BY
SIR GEORGE ABRAHAM GRIERSON
K.C.I.E.

IN THREE PARTS

PART III: SUPPLEMENTARY: ADDITIONS AND CORRECTIONS ETC.
BENGALI INDEX (1971)

London

GEORGE ALLEN & UNWIN LTD

RUSKIN HOUSE MUSEUM STREET

FIRST PUBLISHED BY
GEORGE ALLEN AND UNWIN LTD
1972

ISBN 0 04 491009 6

Photolithography from reproduction pulls by
The Baptist Mission Press, Calcutta,
and by the Shree-Krishna Press, Calcutta (Bengali Index only)

PRINTED IN GREAT BRITAIN BY
LOWE AND BRYDONE (PRINTERS) LTD, LONDON

ADDITIONS AND CORRECTIONS

(Revised to March 1971)

(The numbers refer to pages in the two volumes)

INTRODUCTION

PAGE

1, *l.* 8: the total number of Bengali speakers, after the Partition of India in 1947, was, according to the Census of India for 1961, 33,888,939 persons in West Bengal and India (male 17,610,614, female 16,278,325). In Pakistan (East Bengal), the Bengali speakers numbered 50,853,721 (or 50,840,235 ?). A subsequent estimate for the population of East Bengal in Pakistan was 61 millions. The grand total for Bengali in the subcontinent of India would now be (1970) over 95 millions approximately. Bengali is thus one of the most important languages of the world, both numerically and culturally.

1, *footnote*: the question of 'Hindi' (Hindustani, Hindusthani, High Hindi, Urdu, Khari-Boli, Western Hindi, or 'Hirdu', a composite name, from Hindi +Urdu, created for precise scientific purposes by Ashok R. Kelkar, 'Studies in Hindi and Urdu', Deccan College, Poona, 1968), has now become a political one, and highly controversial, after the first few years of Independence. (See 'Report of the Official Language Commission', Publication Department of the Government of India, New Delhi, 1956, with Notes of Dissent by Suniti Kumar Chatterji and P. Subbaroyan; see also 'Report of the Government of India Sanskrit Commission', New Delhi, 1957.)

According to the 1961 Census, 16,806,772 persons declared their mother tongue as 'Bihari' (which includes Bhojpuri, Sadani, Maithili and Magahi), in addition to 7,964,755 persons who gave as their mother tongue Bhojpuri, 532,000 persons as Sadani (a form of Bhojpuri), 4,984,811 persons as Maithili and 2,818,592 persons as Magahi. Besides, Rajasthani has been given as their mother tongue by 14,493,018 persons, 'Pahari' by 1,004,391 and Garhwali by 1,309,038. And 557,034 people have registered themselves as speakers of Awadhi, 557,034 of Baghelkhandi, and 2,962,038 persons have declared themselves for Chattisgarhi (actually the numbers for these *Kosali*, or so-called 'Eastern Hindi' speeches will be considerably more). These numbers will have to be deducted from 133,435,360 as the figure given for 'Hindi', and 23,323,518 persons who declared for Urdu should, as speakers of Urdu as a 'Western Hindi' speech, be brought under 'Hindi', taking Hindi in its widest sense. There is a growing movement among many of the speakers of what are usually called 'Hindi dialects' to claim for their speeches the status of independent languages, standing on an equal footing with 'Hindi'. Maithili claiming to be the mother tongue of some 15 to 20 millions of people has already been given recognition as an independent language by the Sahitya Akademi, and efforts are being made for Rajasthani and a few more. All this is reducing to a very large extent the numerical superiority claimed for 'Hindi', and from 44 per cent of the Indian people, declared in many quarters as being Hindi-speakers or Hindi-users, the figure has been suggested as 33 per cent, or even 27 per cent, or as low as 25 per cent. But these figures are no more based on accurate data than the much higher figure of 44 per cent.

Of the *Eleven Great Languages of the World*, which are now current among peoples numbering more than 50 millions, the position of Bengali is the *eighth*. Bengali comes after the following:

(1) *Northern Chinese*, which is spoken by some 300 millions in Northern and North-eastern China, and is the official language of nearly 750 millions of the 'Han' or Chinese-speaking China (people who speak what are properly *not Dialects* of a Single Modern Chinese Speech which does not exist, but are really Independent *Languages* derived ultimately from Old Chinese of 2,000 years ago as its modern transformations), besides other peoples of the multilingual Chinese Communist State, like the Tibetans, the Uighur Turks, the Mongols, the Miao-tzes and others.

(2) *English*, the mother tongue of over 250 millions in the United Kingdom and Eire, in the United States of America, in Canada, in New Zealand, in Australia and in the Union of South Africa, and other areas within the former British Empire; and in addition, over 700 millions within the orbit of the former British Empire, in India, in Burma, in Ceylon, in Malaya, in Nigeria, in Ghana and over a great part of Africa and elsewhere, may be described as being still within the domain of English, retaining English to a very large extent as their great administrative, commercial and technological, educational and scientific and cultural language; and the importance of English, as the greatest World Language, reinforced by the position of the United States of America, is extending very rapidly all over the world at the present day, including even the Soviet Union, China, Korea, Japan, the Philippines and Indonesia.

(3) *Hindustani* (*Hindostani*, *Hindusthani*, *Hindi*, *Urdu*, *Bazar Hindi* or *Hindustani*, etc.). It is now the most widely understood language in India, particularly in Northern India, and is current among some 150 to 160 millions as their language of public life, literature and education, industry and business, and of the army, although it is the *home language* of a much smaller number, not more than 60 millions.

(4) *Spanish*, which would cover some 120 millions of people in Spain and Latin America (a large percentage of whom in America speak at home the various Amerindian languages like Aztec and Zapotec, Maya and Chibeha, Quechua and Aymara, Araucanian and Guarani, etc., but they have to learn Spanish at school and are on the way to becoming Spanish speakers).

(5) *Russian or Great Russian* (*Velikorusskiy*), spoken by over 110 millions. It is now the language of higher education and culture, of science and industry and of administration, like English in India, among the 250 millions of the Soviet Union, speaking, in addition to forms of Russian like *Byelorusskiy* or White Russian and *Malorusskiy* or Little Russian (or Ukrainan), various other languages of the Indo-European, Altaic and Finno-Ugrian and other families, like the Baltic speeches of Latvia and Lithuania, Armenian, Ossetic, Persian dialects, Kharthvelian or Georgian, Azerbaijan Turki, the Uighur or Eastern Turki dialects of Central Asia,

Mongol dialects like Khalkha, Buriat and Kalmyk, Esthonian, Kerelian Finnish, Ostyak, Vogul, etc., etc.; and Russian is now acquiring a greater and greater position as an international language of literature and science.

(6) *German*, current among over 100 millions in the Federal and Democratic Republics of Germany, in Austria, in Switzerland, and among groups settled in the Soviet Union and in the Central European States, but maintaining its great importance as a language of science and literature and culture.

(7) *Japanese*, now current among some 100 millions and more, a language with its own place in the scientific and industrial as well as cultural world of today.

(8) *Bengali*, spoken by over 95 millions in India and Pakistan, with its importance as a language of culture and literature, boasting, among other great writers, of Rabindranath Tagore who wrote in Bengali.

(9) *Indonesian*, or *Malay*, spoken in Malaysia, and in the islands of S.E. Asia (Indonesia, Borneo) by some 80 millions.

After these nine, we have to mention two other great languages of the world, numerically not so high in rank as the other ones, but these two have played a conspicuous part in the international domain, as languages of high culture and science, and of religion (in the case of Arabic), namely—

(10) *Arabic*, current among more than 65 millions over a vast area including parts of South-western Iran, Arabia, Iṛaq, Syria, Lebanon, Israel, Egypt, Sudan, the North African States of Tripoli, Tunis, Algeria and Morocco, the Sahara, and parts of Central Africa; and it is studied in all Moslem communities, in Turkey, in the Caucasus regions, in Iran, in Afghanistan, in Pakistan and India, in Central Asia, in China, in Indo-China, in Indonesia, as a sacred language; and finally,

(11) *French*, 55 to 60 millions, in France, Belgium, Switzerland and Canada and in dialectal form (as the Creole speeches) in the former French Colonies in West Africa, in Congo, in Madagascar, in Indo-China, in the West Indies, but still holding its specially important place as an international language of science, letters, culture and commerce.

2, *l*. 4: *correct* 'aboriginal' *to* 'Ādivāsī'.

2, *l.* 16: Robert Shafer has suggested connecting the Lepcha (Lepca or Rong) speech of Darjeeling and Sikkim with the Naga dialect group of Assam, which are members of the Bodo-Naga section of Tibeto-Burman: see R. Shafer, 'Classification of some Languages of the Himalayas', in the 'Journal of the Bihar Research Society', Patna, Vol. XXXVI, 1950, p. 193.

2, *footnote*: Jean Przyluski accepted the term *Kol* side by side with *Munda*: see 'Les Langues du Monde', under the general editorship of Antoine Meillet and Marcel Cohen, Paris, 1924, p. 399. P. O. Bodding, great authority on Santali, thought that the word *Kol* as a monosyllable was 'too naked'. But there are numerous other examples of words of a single syllable as names of languages and peoples: e.g. *Mon, Khmer, Han, Hun, Finn, Thai* (=*Dai*), *Turk, Druz, Hai, Kur, Gwa*, etc. This objection can be met by using, in English and other European languages, derived adjectival forms like *Kolian*, and in Sanskrit and other Indian languages forms like *Kollīya* or *Kolīya*. See further in connexion with Kol, Suniti Kumar Chatterji, 'The Study of Kol' in the 'Calcutta Review', September 1923, pp. 451–73 (subsequently reprinted in the *Visvabharati* Journal for 1924, under the caption 'Our Elder Brothers, the Kols', and elsewhere).

3, *l.* 8 and *l.* 13: *correct* 'aboriginal' *to* 'Ādivāsī'.

4, *top, Section under* 'Dardic, or Piśāca': the classification of the Dardic speeches as made by Georg Morgenstierne of Oslo is to be followed: (*a*) Pašai (Pashai); (*b*) 'Kāfir' Dialects—Katī or Bašgālī, Aškund, Waigeli, Prasūn or Vasi-veron; (*c*) Tirāhī; (*d*) Kalaša; (*e*) Gawar-Batī; (*f*) Khowar or Chitrālī; (*g*) Dialects of Indus Kohistān; (*h*) Šīṇā or Shīṇā Dialects—Gilgitī, Chilasī, Astorī, Gurezī, Brok-pa; and (*i*) Kashmīrī (Kōširī) with Kištawarī.

4, *l.* 13: *read* 1915 *for* 1914, *and* F. *for* W.

4, In the Table for Iranian Languages, beside 'Persic, Avestic, Scythic, and East Iranian', add another group 'South-Eastern Iranian', and place 'Ormuri or Bargišta' and a new name 'Parāchī' under that. 'Paṣto (Pashto)' is to be brought under 'East Iranian' as a separate sub-branch of East Iranian beside the Ghalchah speeches; and 'Balochi' has been suggested (by Tedesco) as being West Iranian, coming under 'Persic', with some Eastern influence. 'Avestic' would then stand isolated, without any living representative.

5, *after line* 22 *add*: It has been suggested that Dialect A of Kuchean was really the spoken language of Tokharistan (= Ferghana area in Central Asia) by the people known as the *Ar-ši* (*Ar-shi*), whom the Greeks called the-*Asianoi*. Then this dialect was taken from Ferghana to Kucha, the seat of Dialect B, as a religious and literary speech (see Sieg and Siegling, 'Tocharische Sprachreste'; and also their articles in the 'Sitzungsberichte der Königlichen Preussichen Akademie der Wissenschaften', before 1939).

6, *add, after line* 2: Quite a literature is now growing up on the Hittite language and the linguistic, historical and other problems that are now cropping up in this connexion. A convenient handbook on Hittite in English is E. H. Sturtevant's 'Comparative Grammar of the Hittite Language', Revised edition, Vol. I, New Haven, U.S.A., 1951; and mention may be made of Suniti Kumar Chatterji's chapter on the Hittite language as in pp. 267–87 of 'Indo-Aryan and Hindi', Second (Revised) edition, Firma K. L. Mukhopadhyay, Calcutta, 1960, reprinted 1969 (Appendix I on 'Pre-Indo-European', first published in 'Indian Culture', Calcutta, VIII, 4, April-June 1942, pp. 309–322); Bata Krishna Ghosh, 'Ancient Languages of Asia Minor', in the 'Indian Culture', 1945, April-June, pp. 147–160; and Satya Swarup Misra's 'Comparative Grammar of Sanskrit, Greek and Hittite', Calcutta, 1968; and his 'The Laryngeal Controversy' in the 'Katre Felicitation Volume', Deccan College, Poona, 1970, pp. 155–177.

Note on Table facing p. 6:

Above 'Kēkaya, Madra, Ṭakka, etc.', put down 'Gāndhārī Prakrit', in line with 'Śaurasēnī, Ardha-māgadhī, Māgadhī and Māhārāṣṭrī'. Similarly, above 'Eḷu', put down 'Sīhaḷa or Siṁhala Prakrit'. The name 'Gāndhārī', for the Early MIA and Prakrit of the North-West, has been suggested by Prof. Sukumar Sen and Prof. H. W. Bailey. The 'Sīhaḷa or Siṁhala Prakrit' is represented mainly by the language of the Sigiriya Graffiti, from the fifth to the eleventh century A.D. The 'Halbi' Language, spoken in Bastar in Madhya Pradesh, is to be placed under Māgadhī Apabhraṁśa (or Ardha-māgadhī Apabhraṁśa) as a separate sub-branch.

Also the 'Bishnupuriyā' speech is to be placed beside Bengali and Assamese under 'Māgadhī Apabhraṁśa'.

7, *Para* 8: Western Panjabi, or Lahnda, or Lahndē-dī-Bōlī, or Lahndī. Another name for this speech has been suggested by Sri Jayachandra Vidyalankara, namely *Hindkī*, which would appear to be most suitable. Dr. Siddheshwar Varma proposed the name *Sindh-Sāgarī* (see 'The Phonetics of Lahnda' by Dr. Siddheshwar Varma, JRASB, Vol. II, 1936, pp. 47–48). 'Gāndhārī Prakrit' should be considered in this connexion. For Lahndi, see Hardev Bahri, 'Lahndi Phonology', 1962, p. 240, and 'Lahndi Phonetics', 1963, p. 292, Loka-bharati, 15A Gandhi Marg, Allahabad.

8, *ll.* 20–23: These voiced stops accompanied by closure of the glottis are as a matter of fact found in certain East Bengali dialects, as regular substitutes for the voiced aspirates (g', dz', ḍ', d', b') for [gɦ, ȷʒɦ, ḍɦ, dɦ, bɦ], as I have found out subsequently. In East Bengali, there is accompanying high tone with glottal closure.

8, *after para* 10, *add*: It would appear, however, that Sindhi in its Apabhraṁśa stage had already a literature prior to A.D. 1000. See Suniti Kumar Chatterji, 'An Early Arabic Version of the Mahābhārata Story', in 'Indian Linguistics', Vol. XI, pts. II–IV, Calcutta 1949–50; and 'An Early Arabic Version of the Mahābhārata Story from Sindh; and Old Sindhi Literature and Culture', in 'Indo-Asian Culture', Indian Institute for Cultural Relations, New Delhi, Vol. VII, No. 1, July 1958, pp. 50–71. Cf. also 'Notes on Early Sindhi Literature', in S. K. Chatterji's 'Languages and Literatures of Modern India', Calcutta, 1963, pp. 341–360.

9, *at the end of para* 11 *on Rajasthani, add*: A little-known language called *Saurāṣṭrī Bhāṣā* is current in the Telugu, Tamil and Malayalam tracts of South India, which is to be considered under Rajasthani. It is spoken by a caste of silk-weavers, called *Paṭa-nūl-kārar* in the Tamil country, numbering some 104,000 persons in Madurai and elsewhere in the Tamil country, of whom 89,000 speak Tamil as their second language. There is a little literature printed in the eighties of the nineteenth century, using the Nagari script. The language is much influenced by Tamil, Telugu and

Marathi, in both vocabulary and grammar. The language is of the Hindi-Gujarati type in morphology, and there is considerable Dravidian influence in syntax. These *Saurāṣṭrī* speakers are supposed to be descended from silk-weavers (*Paṭṭa-vāyas*) of the Mandasor Inscription of c. A.D. 437–438, belonging originally to *Lāṭa-viṣaya* or Gujarat, whence in the fourteenth century they migrated to Devagiri or Daulatabad in the Maratha country, and then passed through Vijayanagara to the Tamil country, with their headquarters now in Madurai. See *Paṭnūlī*, 'Linguistic Survey of India', Vol. IX, Part 2, pp. 447–448; H. N. Randle, 'An Indo-Aryan Language of South India', in the BSOAS, University of London, Vol. XI, 1943–46, pp. 104–121, 310–327. The speakers of this language in the Tamil Country are making a desperate attempt to preserve it.

10, *l.* 4 *from below*: *after* 'Bendall and Conrady', *add*: Suniti Kumar Chatterji, article in the VSPdP for Bengali Year 1336, Vol. XXXVI, No. 3; '"Nepālē Bhāṣā-nāṭak"-sambandhē Mantavya'; and 'Gopīcandra Nāṭaka', a seventeenth-century Bengali play from Nepal —now edited from the Cambridge MS. with introduction, notes and glossary, in the Roman character, by Tarapada Mukherji, SOAS, London, from the University of Calcutta, 1970.

11, *l.* 17: *Correct dates to* A.D. 1089–1173.

12, *l.* 14, *after* 'in the Deccan', *add*: (The oldest work of this type available is the Sufi treatise *Mirāju-l-'Āšiqīn* by Sayyid Muhammad Banda-nawāz Gēsū-darāz, who died in A.D. 1442).

12, *ll.* 12–17: Amir Khusrau was born at Patiyali in 1253, and died in Delhi in 1325 (E. G. Browne, 'Literary History of Persia', London, Vol. II, p. 540). The first authentic poet of Urdu seems to have been Muhammad Quli Qutb Šāh, king of Golconda in the Deccan, who died in A.D. 1611 He used a vernacular Western Hindi speech with Panjabi affinities, not exactly identical with the Hindostani of later times (cf. Braj-ratn Dās, 'Urdū-kā Pratham Kavi' in the 'Nagari Pracarini Patrika', Benares, New Series, Vol. 4, No. 2).

12, *l.* 22: *add, after* establishment of Hindostani: (cf. 'Urdū: the name and the Language' by T. Grahama Bailey in the JRAS, London, April 1930, pp. 391–400. Bailey definitely declares that Urdu is derived out of 'Old

Panjabi' of Lahore, from 1027 when Mahmud of Ghazna annexed the Panjab. The 'Old Khaṛī-Bōlī' of Delhi then considerably modified it. This is also the view put forward by Prof. Mahmud Shirani of Lahore in his 'Panjāb-mẽ Urdū', Lucknow, Maktaba-i-Kalian, 1960).

13, *after l.* 19, *add a new paragraph*: The question of Dakni in the evolution of Urdu and Hindustani is an important one. Dakni literature is now being studied by both scholars of Urdu (notably the late Dr. Saiyad Mohiuddin Qadrī 'Zōr', † September 24, 1962, and Prof. Masud Husain Khan of the Aligarh Muslim University) and of Hindi (like Dr. Sriram Sarma, author of 'Dakkhinī Hindī-kā Udbhav aur Vikās', Hindi Sahitya Sammelan, Allahabad, 1964, and other works), and a considerable mass of Dakni literature has been made available in print in both Urdu and Nagari scripts. A new light is being thrown through these studies on the origin and development of Hindi-Urdu as different forms of the same Protean North Indian speech.

13, *ll.* 22 *ff.*: The figures, as for most other Indian languages of the North, are only approximate. The proper name for 'Eastern Hindi', as suggested, should be 'Kosalī', with three main dialects, Awadhī (or Baiswāḍī), Baghēlī (or Baghēlkhaṇḍī) and Chhattisgaṛhī. The earliest specimens of Awadhī or Kosalī are in the *Uktivyakti-prakaraṇa* of Dāmōdara, which was composed during the first half of the thirteenth century. This is a work teaching Sanskrit through a New Indo-Aryan speech, and that speech is 'Old Kosali' (see Grammatical Introduction by Suniti Kumar Chatterji to the edition of the 'Ukti-vyakti-prakaraṇa' by Muni Jinavijayaji in the 'Singhi Jain Series', No. 39, Bombay, 1953).

13, *add at the end*:

Some speakers of Awadhi are looking forward to the rehabilitation of Awadhi as an independent language beside Hindi and Urdu. The Early Awadhi tradition in literature is still living (witness a work like *Dēhrā-Dūn* by the late Sridhar Pathak, and the epic *Kṛṣṇāyana*, of 906 pages, in the style of Tulasidasa's *Rāmacarita-mānasa*, by Dwarkaprasad Misra, Lucknow, 1946). For a comprehensive historical study of Awadhi, see Baburam Saksena's pioneer work, 'the Evolution of Awadhi', Allahabad, 1938, and Uday Narayan Tiwari's book in Hindi, 'Hindī-bhāṣā-kā

Udgam aur Vikāś', Allahabad, Saṃvat 2012 = 1956, pp. 268 ff. See also Bhalachandra Rao Telang, 'Chattīsgaṛhī, Halbī, Bhatrī Bōliyõ-kā Bhāṣā-Vaijñānik Adhyayan', Hindi-Granth-Ratnākar Private Ltd., Hirabagh, Bombay-4, 1966, p. 616.

One of the sub-dialects of Kosali is the *Gahorā* form of the Bagheli dialect, now current in East Banda district to the south of the Jamna (Yamunā) river: cf. LSI, VI, p. 150. This is virtually the same as Awadhi. The name *Gahorā* (or *Gahorī*) appears to have been taken to distant East Bengal by Muslim Sufi missionaries and teachers (from Eastern U.P. of the present day), who introduced Sufi literature in Awadhi (like the *Lōr-Candā* romance of Mullā Dā'ūd, *c.* A.D. 1375 and the *Padumāwat* of Malik Muhammad Jāyasī, *c.* 1545) which was studied by Bengali Muslims in Chittagong and imitated or adapted by them in Bengali from the seventeenth century onwards; and this name of a sub-dialect of Kosali was extended by East Bengal Muslim writers to mean the Eastern Hindi or Kosali speech of Malik Muhammad Jāyasī and others, and was called by them *Gohārī* (or *Goārī*) *Bhāṣā*.

Awadhi literature has a long history, from the thirteenth century onwards (the *Ukti-vyakti-prakaraṇa*). Before Malik Muhammad Jāyasī and Tulasidasa (second half of the sixteenth century), we have a succession of Sufi writers, beginning with Mullā or Maulānā Dā'ūd, who wrote (*c.* A.D. 1375) his *Candāyan* or Romance of Lor and Chanda; and between Maulānā Dā'ūd and Malik Muhammad Jāyasī we have to mention Kutban (wrote *Mrigāvati*, *c.* A.D. 1501), Manjhan (*c.* 1532: *Madhu-Mālati*), and a number of other poets in the seventeenth and eighteenth centuries. This Awadhi Sufi literature influenced Muslim Bengali literature in the seventeenth and eighteenth centuries.

14. *after para 15, add in continuation*: We have also to mention among the thirteenth- and fourteenth-century writings in Marathi the earliest religious compositions of teachers of the Mahānubhāva (or Mānbhāv) sect, like the Ācārya-sūtra', the 'Siddhānta-sūtra-pāṭha' (Sayings and Teachings of Cakradhara, *c.* A.D. 1263–1271, the founder of the Mahānubhāva sect, collected by his disciple Mahīndra Bhaṭa), the 'Līlā-carita' (or a biography of Cakradhara by Mahīndra Bhaṭa), and the 'Śiśupāla-vadha'

(by Bhāskarācārya, another disciple of Cakradhara, the first truly important literary work in Marathi).

16, *after line* 3, *under* § 18 (Sinhalese), *add*:

'Echo-words' in Sinhalese show a Western Indian (Gujarati and Marathi) basis for Sinhalese as an Indo-Aryan language: see *post*, p. 72, footnote, and also p. 176. Wilhelm Geiger ('A Grammar of the Sinhalese Language', RAS Ceylon Branch, Colombo, 1938, pp. VI ff.) is for the affiliation of Sinhalese to a Western Indian Prākrit, and he criticizes the view put forward by Rambukwele Siddhartha and Muhammad Shahidullah regarding the supposed Eastern Indian affinities of Sinhalese. The Eastern origin of Sinhalese has been supported also by P. B. F. Wijeratne (in his 'Phonology of the Sinhalese Inscriptions up to the end of the Tenth Century A.D.', in the BSOAS, London, XI, 1943–46, pp. 580 ff., especially 'Introduction', pp. 587 ff.). But in this connexion, it may be questioned how far the language of the inscriptions from the third century B.C. represents the actual spoken language of the Aryan settlers in Ceylon, and how far it is merely an artificial composite speech for specific epigraphic purposes.

16, *add, at the end of para 19 on the Gipsy Dialects of Europe*: 'The Dialect of the Gipsies of Wales' by John Sampson, Oxford University Press, 1926, is a most important work dealing with the Gipsy speech in its Indo-Aryan background. See also Ralph L. Turner, 'The Position of Romani in Indo-Aryan', in the 'Journal of the Gipsy Lore Society', 3rd series, Vol. 5, No. 4, 1926, pp. 145–89. Cf. also C. J. Poppa-Serboianu, 'Les Tsiganes: Histoire, Ethnographie, Linguistique, Grammaire, Dictionnaire', Paris, 1930. Serboianu deals with Rumanian Gipsies, and he computes the total number of Gipsies in the world at five millions: see p. 35, *op. cit.*

18, *l.* 11, *correct* 'A.C.' *to* 'B.C.'

21, *l.* 9, *use* 'Bhojpurī' *for* 'Bhojpuriyā'.

l. 24, *after* « -abba- », *add* as well as the present participle in « -ant- ».

l. 25, *after the word* tense *within the brackets add*: even of the transitive verbs, which uniformly developed later from a passive construction in MIA.

22, *l.* 9: *after* Poona, 1918 *within brackets, add,* Jules Bloch, 'L' Indo-Aryen du Veda aux Temps Modernes', Paris, 1934; Suniti Kumar Chatterji, 'Indo-Aryan and Hindi', 2nd Edition, Firma K. L. Mukhopadhyay, Calcutta, 1960, reprinted 1969; T. Burrow, 'The Sanskrit Language', London, 1955.

24, *l.* 16: *After* Indo-European home, *add*: The latest and quite a convincing opinion has been expressed by W. Brandenstein, who by a close study of the ancient Indo-European languages has come to the conclusion that the history of the IE speech can be divided into two strata, of which the first stratum was developed or characterized in the dry hilly tracts and plains to the south of the Ural Mountains, in Eurasia, and the second stratum was developed in the moister lands of Eastern Europe, corresponding to the present-day Poland (W. Brandenstein, 'Die Erste Wanderungen der IG Völker', 1936, of which a résumé in English from A. Berriedale Keith appeared in the 'Indian Historical Quarterly' Calcutta, Vol. XIII, 1, March 1937).

25, *l.* 21: *continue, within brackets*: See also Walter Porzig 'Klein-Asiatisch-Indische Beziehungen' in the 'Zeitschrift für Indologie und Iranistik', Band V, Heft. 3, 1927, pp. 265 ff. It has been suggested by Porzig that a number of Asianic words were picked up by the Aryans in Asia Minor, among which may be mentioned the Sanskrit word for 'grape' = « drākṣā < drāk-sā », from « *dherg(h), *tereg », whence Lydian « targanon » *sour wine*, Greek « truks », genitive « trugos » *sweet wine*, etc., and « kūpa » *well, cave.* Cf. also S. K. Chatterji, 'Dravidian Origins and the Beginnings of Indian Civilization' in the 'Modern Review', December 1924, and also 'The Foundations of Civilization in India' in the 'Tijdschrift van Koninglijk Bataviaasch Genootschap van Kunst en Watenschappen', LXVIII, Batavia, 1928.

26, *footnote*: P. T. Srinivas Iyengar *for* P. Srinivas Iyengar.

27, *l.* 16, *add at the end*: see, S. K. Chatterji, the paper on Dravidian Origins, mentioned above; and also S. K. Chatterji, 'Dravidian', Annamalai University, Annamalainagar, Tamil-Nad, 1965, pp. 32 ff.

27, *l.* 17: *after* 1916, p. 364, *add*: R. G. Bhandarkar, in the JBBRAS, Vol. 25, 1917, pp. 76–81.

28, *footnote, l.* 10: *in the list of references on the Harappa seals, add at the beginning*: A. Cunningham (Archaeological) Reports, Vol. 5 (1875), pp. 105 ff.; J. F. Fleet, JRAS, 1912, pp. 699 ff.

About the recent discoveries in Sindh and at Harappa, see Sir John Marshall's article in the 'Illustrated London News' for September 20, 1924, and further articles by Prof. A. H. Sayce and Messrs. C. J. Gadd and Sidney Smith in the same journal for September 27 and October 4, 1924, respectively. Cf. also S. K. Chatterji, 'Dravidian Origins and the Beginnings of Indian Civilisation' in the 'Modern Review' for December 1924; also the 'Modern Review' for February 1925, and the 'Journal Asiatique' for 1925, p. 371. See also 'Sumerian connexions with Ancient India', by Ernest Mackay, JRAS for 1925, pp. 697–701. Further articles on these 'Indo-Sumerian' antiquities by Sir John Marshall have appeared in the 'Illustrated London News' for February 17 and March 6, 1926, and in the 'Times of India Illustrated Weekly' for March 7, 1926. In 1931 appeared Sir John Marshall's *magnum opus* (in collaboration with others) on 'Mohen-jo-Daro and the Indus Civilisation', 3 Vols., London. This was followed by 'Further Excavations at Mohen-jo-Daro', by E. Mackay and others (Delhi, 1938), and 'Excavations at Harappa' by Madhav Swarup Vats and others (2 Vols., Delhi, 1940). See also Stuart Piggott, 'Prehistoric India to 1000 B.C.', Pelican Books A205, 1950; Bridget and Raymond Allchin, 'The Birth of Indian Civilisation: India and Pakistan before 500 B.C.', Penguin Books A905, 1968; D. H. Gordon, 'The Prehistoric Background of Indian Culture', Bhulabhai Memorial Institute, Bombay, 1958; and Heinz Mode, 'Die Frühe Indien', Gustav Kilpper Verlag, Stuttgart, 1959. By now (1970) quite a literature has grown up on the Indus Valley Civilization and its script, and the ramifications of this civilization in other parts of India, like Lothal in Gujarat and Rupar in North-eastern Panjab.

Attempts are being made internationally to read the ancient Indus Valley script, and this has become quite an important branch of Indology. The latest advance appears to have been made during past few years by a team of Soviet (Russian) scholars using computers in the analysis of the Indus Valley writing, whose methods have been accepted by a team of

Finnish scholars (Asko Parpola and others, working in Copenhagen), and by the Indian scholar Iravathan Mahadeven, whose papers are now before the public (1970). The language is now considered to be Dravidian.

28, *footnote, l.* 3 *from bottom*: *correct* 'Krishna' *to* 'Kentish'.

29, *ll.* 11, 12: The statements made here are to be modified. The Austric Kōl or Muṇḍā people supplied one of the main bases in the formation of the Indo-Aryan speaking masses in Northern India, particularly, in the Ganges Valley, and the bed-rock of Indian or Hindu economic and social life in the villages is largely of Kōl origin. Agriculture, both the primitive form of it with the digging stick (*jhoom* cultivation) and with the hoe or spade (as still current in Nepal), and the advanced form with the plough (*lāngala*) and oxen, the cultivation of rice and of some of the millets, use of some vegetables like the pumpkin (*alābu*) and the brinjal (*bātiṅgana*), and fruits like the banana (*kadalī*) and the jack-fruit (*panasa*) and some condiments like the turmeric (*haridrā*), the mustard (*sarṣapa*), the pepper (*pippalī*) and the ginger (*śṛṅgavēra*), as well as spinning and weaving of cloth from cotton (*kārpāsa*), besides the raising of the domestic fowl and the pig, the taming of the elephant, and observance of great seasonal festivals, were in all likelihood derived from Kōl or Muṇḍā culture. The horse or pony (*sada, sadom*) was also known to them. See in this connexion Sarat Chandra Roy's 'The Mundas and their Country', Calcutta and Ranchi, 1912; J. Hoffmann, 'Encyclopaedia Mundarica', 14 Parts, Patna Government Press, 1914–1919; Suniti Kumar Chatterji, 'The Study of Kōl', 'Calcutta Review', 1923; Sylvain Lévi, Jean Przyluski and Jules Bloch, 'Pre-Aryan et Pre-Dravidian dans l'Inde', English Translation by Prabodh Chandra Bagchi (with additional notes by S. K. Chatterji and P. C. Bagchi), University of Calcutta, 1929; F. B. J. Kuiper, 'Austro-Asiatic Words in Sanskrit', London, 1950; Suniti Kumar Chatterji, 'Indianism and the Indian Synthesis', Kamala Lectures for 1947, University of Calcutta, 1962.

30, *ll.* 6, 7: This statement also is to be modified, when we think of the great culture of at least some of the Tibeto-Chinese peoples of India like the Newars of Nepal and the Meitheis of Manipur, as well as the Bodo peoples of Assam and Tipperah and the Ahoms of Assam. See in this connexion

Suniti Kumar Chatterji, '*Kirata-jana-kṛti*: the Indo-Mongoloids—their Contribution to the History and Culture of India', the Asiatic Society, Calcutta, 1951; and also S. K. Chatterji's 'Religious and Cultural Integration of India: Atombapu Sarma of Manipur', Paṇḍita-rāja Gaveshaṇā Kēndra, Imphal, Manipur, 1967.

30, *before para* **29**, *add a new section:* **28a**:

Of the various pre-Aryan peoples who lived in India before the Aryans came, we have to take note, in the first instance, of the Dravidians. In all likelihood, it was the Dravidian speakers who had built up the city civilizations of Mohen-jo-Daro and Harappa and other culture centres in Northern and North-Western India. Probably Dravidians were also spread in North India as much as in South India, and a good deal of the religious ideals as well as of the general civilization and way of life of the Dravidians, as that of a highly advanced group of people in India, furnished some of the most important bases to the composite Hindu civilization of India. In addition to the Dravidians, we have also the Austric (Austro-Asiatic) people—the Kōl (or Kolian, or Muṇḍā) as well as Mon-Khmer branches of which were living in Northern India; and probably the Austrics had penetrated also right down to the extreme southern parts of India. The Austrics do not appear to have evolved a city culture, like that of the Dravidians. But the bases of the village culture of India established on the cultivation of rice, and on many other matters of vital importance in civilized and corporate life, were evolved among the Austrics. The Sino-Tibetan speaking Mongoloids are at present found along the Himalayan regions, and in Assam and North and East Bengal. But at one time they appear to have penetrated down to Central India, and as far south as South Rajasthan (Kirāḍū). They do not appear to have advanced very far in material civilization. But nevertheless, they have furnished important racial as well as linguistic and religious and other elements in the evolution of the Indian people. In addition to these four basic racial groups (or, to be non-committal, 'language-culture' groups) in India, namely Aryan and Dravidian, Austric and Mongoloid (or, to give their Sanskrit names, *Ārya*, *Dramiḍa* or *Drāviḍa*, *Niṣāda* and *Kirāta*, respectively), it is not unlikely that there was one (or were there more than one?)

ethnic or language-culture group (or groups), the identity as well as affinity of which is now lost. These pre-Aryan tribes appear to have lived mostly in Central India. T. Burrow and Sudhi Bhushan Bhattacharya suggested that some unknown linguistic group (or groups), apart from the four mentioned above, was responsible for an unexplained element of vocabulary in Indian languages, which cannot be properly relegated to either Aryan or Dravidian, or to Austric or Sino-Tibetan: see Sudhi Bhushan Bhattacharya, 'Field-Notes on Nahali', in the Taraporewala Memorial Volume, 'Indian Linguistics', Vol. 17, 1955–56, June 1957, p. 257; T. Burrow, 'The Sanskrit Language', London, 1956, pp. 376, 377; also T. Burrow, 'Sanskrit and the pre-Aryan Tribes and Languages', 'Bulletin of the Ramakrishna Mission Institute of Culture', Calcutta, Vol. IX, No. 2, February 1968, pp. 34–45, esp. pp. 37, 38, 40, 41, 42, 43. But F. B. J. Kuiper in his 'Nahali: a Comparative Study', Amsterdam, 1962, pp. 11, 15, enjoins caution in this respect.

It is exceedingly likely that the various races of people with their diverse languages, Dravidian, Austric and Mongoloid, and possibly also some unknown people or peoples, gradually began to be welded into one single people when they began to live side by side on the plains of North India. This racial fusion evidently was going hand in hand with a linguistic fusion, when the Aryan language gradually came to be adopted by the various non-Aryan groups, as they were in the need of some common speech. Racial fusion by what are known as *Anulōma* and *Pratilōma* marriages began early enough, and the Sanskrit word *varṇa* or 'colour', to mean a separate group or entity in a social conglomerate, would originally appear to have its basis in colour or complexion in the physical types of the basic component groups—the brown or tawny Dravidian, the dark or black Austric, the yellow or golden Mongoloid and the white or fair Aryan (see 'Contributions from different Language and Culture Groups' by Suniti Kumar Chatterji in the 'Cultural Heritage of India', New Edition, Vol. I, pp. 76–90, Ramakrishna Mission Institute of Culture, Calcutta, 1958). A composite people like this in North India found a common language in the speech of the Aryan, as it was brought into India by this latest ethnic intrusion into India. Out of this fusion emerged, as

F. W. Thomas has put it, 'the Indian Man, who came into being at the end of the Vedic age' ('The Expansion of Indianism' by F. W. Thomas, University of Calcutta, 1941). This 'Indian Man' now mainly spoke the Aryan language (and also Dravidian), but this language was rapidly undergoing a change on the soil of India under altered conditions; and the line of this change and its history is the history of IA in its successive periods of OIA, MIA and NIA, including Bengali.

This great fact of racial, cultural and linguistic miscegenation has always to be taken note of as the background, and a full appraisement of this situation will enable us to find out and appreciate the development of IA through the last 3,000 years. Its history, prior to the advent of the Aryans in India in a pre-Aryan *milieu*, is a different story, although in the Aryan inheritance we have to consider elements received from other races and languages. But all that is a little remote in considering the development of a NIA language like Bengali.

31, *l.* 7: *read* dialects *for* languages.

38, *footnote*: *add*: The study of the Dravidian Languages, Old and New, now being pursued with such conspicuous brilliance by a number of scholars both Indian and European and American, like Alfred Master, L. V. Ramaswami Ayyar, T. Burrow, M. B. Emeneau, Bh. Krishnamurti, Kamil Zvelebil, M. S. Andronov, S. Rudin, Yuri Glasov, T. N. Srikanthayya, V. I. Subramoniam, K. Mahadeva Sastri, Iravathan Mahadevan and others is helping us to reconstruct the pre-history of Dravidian in its various stages like Primitive Dravidian and its branching off into the various forms like North, Central, Eastern and Southern Dravidian.

44, *l.* 16: *correct* Kauṣītakī *to* Kauṣitakī.

44, *l.* 21: *after* p. 387, *add*: cf. also 'the Śatapatha-Brāhmaṇa', III, 2, 3, 15: 'Speech sounds higher here among the Kuru-Pañcālas' (. . . atrôttarā hi vāg vadati Kuru-Pañcālatrā . . .).

44, *l.* 2 *from bottom*: *after* Pali « nahāpita », *add* « khulla *kṣulla, < *kṣudla = kṣudra; naṭa < nṛtu; paṭh < *pṛth, prath: ghaṭ, gaṭh < grath », etc.

46, *l.* 8: The Vrātyas. Mm. Haraprasād Śāstri derives « vrātya » from « vrāta » = *horde*, in a suggestive paper containing some interesting information about 'the Vrātyas or the Original Inhabitants of Magadha', one of six lectures on 'Magadhan Literature', delivered in the University of Patna, 1923; see also his 'Absorption of the Vrātyas', Dacca University Bulletin, No. 6, 1926, and his Bengali article 'Vrātya' in the 'Prācī', Agrahāyaṇa, 1330 B.Y.

47, *l.* 12–21; « hēlayaḥ (hēlavaḥ) ». This form has been sought to be explained as a Semitic word, the same as the Hebrew « 'eloah » = Arabic « 'ilāh » (K. P. Jayaswal, in the ZDMG, Vol. 68, p. 719: cf. R. G. Bhandarkar in the JBBRAS, Vol. 25, pp. 76 ff.). But this is extremely unlikely. Hebrew (as well as Arabic) was rather removed from the tracts where the Aryans moved much or were settled in, in North Mesopotamia and North-Western Iran, at this early period (2000 B.C.–1300 B.C.); and Hebrew conquest of Palestine took place during the closing centuries of the second millennium B.C. The Semitic word for 'god' which the Aryans would be likely to pick up, if they did pick it up at all, would be the Babylonian and Assyrian « ilu », which makes the connexion with the Indian form remote. Jayaswal also derives the Indian « mlēccha (Pkt. milakkhu) » *foreigner* from a Semitic word « m-l-k », in Hebrew « melex » *king*. But there is no reason not to regard this word as Indo-European, as being from « mlaikṣa » *mixed* (see Uhlenbeck, 'Altindisches Etymologisches Wörterbuch'). Iravathan Mahadevan, in his studies of the Mohen-jo-Daro script and languages, sees in « mlēccha » a Sanskritization of the name which was current among the Dravidian-speaking Mohen-jo-Daro people for themselves or for one of their ruling classes.

48, *l.* 27: *add, after* in their meaning: These new words were either morphological extensions of the old ones, or were borrowings from non-Aryan and other extra Indo-Aryan sources.

49, *l.* 3: *add, after* « prastara » (= *stone,* NIA « patthar, pāthar », originally, *rushes spread out,* as in the Yajur-Veda).

51, *after l.* 13, Certain popular or vernacular (MIA) variations of pronunciation and morphology were known and tolerated by Panini: cf. Vidhusekhara Sastri (Bhattacharya), 'Pāṇini-Vyākaraṇa O Saṁskṛte Prākṛta-Prabhāva' in the Bengali Journal 'Pravāsī' for Āṣāḍha, 1341, pp. 307 ff. (Pāṇini, VI, 1, 54; VI, 1, 95; VII, 3, 17; VIII, 3, 26, 27, etc.—the pronunciation of

« hm, hn » as « mh, nh », wrong *sandhi*, intrusive « y- » to prevent a hiatus, etc.).

54, *l.* 33: *after* « -āni », *add*: the dative plural affix was « -ēhi » (= ēbhyaḥ, *-ēbhiḥ) rather than the genitive-dative affix « -ānaṃ » (= ānām) which characterized the Midland, North-Western and Southern speeches as in the Asoka Inscriptions and in Pali (cf. Surendranath Majumdar Sastri, 'The Dative in Pali', in 'Sir Asutosh Mookerjee Silver Jubilee Volumes', III, Calcutta University, 1925).

The following tables of declension will indicate the situation:

	Sanskrit (OIA)	*Pali* (*Śūrasēna*, Midland)
Nom.	rasaḥ—rasāḥ, rasāsaḥ	rasō—rasā
Acc.	rasam—rasān	rasaṃ—rasē, rasān
Ins.	rasēna, rasā—rasāiḥ, rasēbhiḥ	rasēna—rasēhi
Dative	rasāya—rasēbhyaḥ	as for genitive
Genitive	rasasya—rasānām	rasassa—rasānaṃ
Locative	rasē, *rasasmin—rasēṣu	rasē, rasamhi—rasēsu

	Ardha-magadhi (*Kōsala*)	*Magadhi* (East, *Magadha*)
Nom.	lasē—lasā	laśē—laśā, laśāśē
Acc.	lasaṃ—lasāni	laśaṃ—laśāni
Ins.	lasēna—lasēhi	laśā, laśēna—laśēhi
Dative	lasāya—lasēhi	laśāya—laśēhi
Genitive	lasassa—lasānaṃ	laśaśśa—laśānaṃ
Locative	lasassi—lasēsu	laśāśśi—laśēśu

56, *l.* 3: *read* 'presents' *for* 'present'; *and in l.* 19, *read* 'dramas' *for* 'drama'.

57, *l.* 10: The word *Pāli* means 'that which protects', i.e. preserves the texts relating to the Dharma and its interpretation, or texts relating to matters of value. (« dhammatthān pālētī ti pāli; atthān pāti rakkhatī ti tasmā pāli; sadatthān pālētī ti pāli »).

57, *ll.* 24 *ff.* 'Based on a Midland speech . . .'

Mathurā is in the heart of the Midland, and the importance of Mathurā in the organization as well as spread of Buddhism (as well as Jainism) during the centuries round about Christ has been noted. The first images of Buddha, in the native Indian art tradition (apart from the Greco-Indian tradition of Gandhāra art), were made in Mathurā. Cf. J. Przyluski, 'Asokāvadāna', 1923, p. 9: 'l' église de Mathura eût parmi les communautés bouddhiques une situation privilegiée et qu'elle eût pour une large part un rayonnement de la foi'; cf. also Nalinaksha Dutta, 'Spread of Buddhism, mainly based on the Nikāyas', Calcutta University, 1925, Book II, Chapter III, pp. 249–65, specially pp. 254 ff.

59, *l.* 17: *read* nama *for* nāma.

59, *footnote*: Cf. K. P. Jayaswal in the JBORS for 1924, pp. 189 ff. for further Brahmi seals from Magadha with « -śa(= -śśa) » for the genitive affix « -sya » (e.g. Mamaśa, Citaśa, Bhadaṁta Lopagoraśa, Abhaya-vamaśa).

65, *l.* 19: *read* Mōlāḍandī *for* Mōḍālandī.

66, *l.* 6: *from bottom, read* চুঁচুড়া *for* চুচুড়া.

66, *l.* 6: *add at the end*: Assamese জোল « jōl » *water*, জুলিয়া « juliyā » *watery.*

67, *l.* 27: *read* Bāgădis *for* Bāgŭdis (The « Vāthurīs » are different from the « Bāurīs »).

68, *l.* 24: *read* Mangalore *for* Bangalore.

69, *l.* 13: À propos the names « Siam, Sham, Ahom < Rham », see S. K. Chatterji, 'The Name "Assam-Ahom"' in the JAS, Vol. XXII, Letters No. 2, 1956, pp. 147–53.

71, *l.* 4: *read Gaina for* Gaina.

71, *after line* 21, *add*: We have in the 'Dharma-maṅgala' of Ghanarām Chakravarti, Vaṅgavāsī edition, Bengali Year 1308, p. 223: Lakhāi says to Māhudyā or Mahāmada: জাতি রাঢ় আমি রে, করমে রাঢ় তু « jāti rāḍha āmi rē, karamē rāḍha tu »—*I am Rāḍha by caste, you are so by your action.* Compare also 'Bihar Peasant Life', by Sir George Abraham Grierson, first edition 1885, p. 328, the Bihar proverb : « Kaēth kichu lēlē dēlē, barāmhan khiyaulē; dhān, pān paniyaulē, au Rāḍ jāti latiyaulē » '*a Kayasth* (*thrives*) *in some business transaction, a Brahman when he is feasted; paddy and betel-vines, through watering; and a man of the Rāḍh caste* (*he works only*) *when he gets kicked*'.

72, *footnote* : *l.* 2: *read* Lāḷa *for* Laḷa. *Also in l.* 11, *correct* Dipa *to* Dīpa.

73, *footnote*: Rāma-candra Kavi-bhāratī, fifteenth century (*c.* 1434), was received in Ceylon by King Parākrama-bāhu and settled down there, and wrote his well-known Sanskrit work of faith in Buddha the 'Bhakti-Śataka'.

75-76: King Candra-varman of Puṣkaraṇā. The late K. N. Dikshit, of the Archaeological Survey of India, definitely suggested the identification of Puṣkaraṇā of the Susunia Rock Inscription with a place in Bengal—in the district of Bankura, and not with Pokharan in Rajputana. Also Sri Nikhil Nath Ray, B.L., in the 'Bhārata-varṣa' for Jyaiṣṭha, 1330, p. 832. There is actually in that district a village 'Pokharnā' (*vulgo* 'Pakhannā, Pokhannā') on the Damodar river, some 25 miles east of Susunia Hill (23° N 87° E, Bengal Survey, scale one inch = one mile, Sheet No. 238, Survey Season 1854–64). This is conclusive, and it would show that Rāḍha at least was entirely Aryanized, and had a Hindu Vaishnava king in the fourth century A.C.; and it may be concluded that Aryanization was already some centuries old. See also Suniti Kumar Chatterji, Article in the 'Vaṅga-śrī' for Phālguna, 1339 Bengali Year, pp. 135-36: 'Prācīn Vaṅgēr Puṣkaraṇā-Janapad'.

86, *footnote, l.* 3: It is to be noted that the name of the famous town of « Pratiṣṭhāna » in northern Maharashtra, which was in all likelihood Old Kannada in its local speech 2,000 years ago, became « *Paiṭṭhāna » with loss of intervocalic « -t- » as early as the first century B.C., as we can see from the Greek transcription of the name in the 'Periplus of the Erythraean Sea', as « Paithana ».

90, *l.* 19: *add at the end, after* January 1923, *the following*: C. D. Dalal and P. D. Gune, 'Bhavisayatta-kaha by Dhanapāla', Baroda, 1923, Introduction.

94, *ll.* 18–20: the future in « -t- », from the old present participle, occurs in East Vanga Dialects: see under *Morphology*, pp. 961–63.

99: *after l.* 5: Of the Modern Magadhan languages, three have already been studied with great detail from a comparative and historical point: (1) Assamese, by Banikanta Kakati—'Assamese: its Formation and Development', first edition 1941, second edition revised and edited by Golok Chandra Goswami, Gauhati, 1962; (2) Maithili, by Subhadra Jha, 'The Formation of the Maithili Language', London, Luzac & Co., 1958, p.638; and (3) Bhojpuri, by Uday Narayan Tiwari, 'The Origin and Development of the Bhojpuri Language', Asiatic Society, Calcutta, 1960, and his book in Hindi, 'Bhojpurī Bhāṣā aur Sāhitya', Bihar Rashtrabhasha Parishad, Patna, 1954 (besides A. F. Rudolf Hoernle's 'Comparative

Grammar of the Gaudian Languages with special reference to Eastern Hindi' i.e. Bhojpuri, London, 1880). Comparative and historical studies in Oriya and Magahi have also started. Mention may be made of the papers on 'A Historical Phonology of Oriya' by Paresh Chandra Majumdar, published in the Indological Journal 'Our Heritage', Government Sanskrit College, Calcutta, Vol. XII, pt. I, 1964 and Vol. XIV, pt. I, 1966, and Kaliprasad Sinha's doctorate thesis on the 'Vishnupriyā' (Bishnupuriyā) Speech for the University of Jadavpur, Calcutta. These books and papers are now indispensable for the study of the Magadhan languages.

99, *after line* 16: Some short stories and poems are occasionally published in Bhojpuri, and a few short novels and comic sketches in prose have also appeared, besides some dramas by the late Rahul Sankrityayana. At least one journal advocating the revival of Bhojpuri came into existence about two decades ago, but it has now stopped. A second journal, now in its tenth year, the 'Ā̃jōr', edited by Pandeya Narmadeswar Sahay and published by 'the Bhojpuri Pariwār', Patna 1, is now coming out regularly, in which poems, short stories and general articles, all in Bhojpuri, are published. There is also another literary journal in Bhojpuri, the 'Bhojpuri Kahāniyā̃', editor Sri Rambalī Pāṇḍeya, published by the Bhojpuri Samsad, Jagatganj, Varanasi, now (July 1969) in its fifth year, which is an active champion of Bhojpuri. The Samsad also has a quarterly journal, the 'Purabaiyā'. Some eight social films, all in pure Bhojpuri, like the 'Gaṅgā-Maiyā tohē piyariyā caḍhaibau' and 'Hamār Sansār', have appeared during the present decade, and these draw enthusiastic Bhojpuri-speaking audiences in all the towns of Northern and Eastern India. Then there is the very popular song-drama, the 'Bidesiyā Nāṭak' by a distinguished poet of Bhojpuri, Bhikhārī Ṭhākur, which Bhojpuri speakers all over Bihar and U.P. and in Calcutta and elsewhere gather in large numbers to witness and listen to the songs. This 'Bidesiyā Nāṭak' has been printed.

100, *l.* 6: *for* rahaulaũ, *read* rahalaũ.

102, *l.* 7: Grierson published the Magahi Text of 'the Birth of Lorik' in the BSOS, V (1928–30), pp. 591–99. The late Jainath Pati, *Mukhtar* of Nawadah (Gaya), wrote and published two small social novels in Magahi, 'Sunītā' and 'Phūl-Bahādur'. A journal in Magahi called the 'Bihān' (*Dawn*) continues to be published from Patna (October 1969). A good collection of Magahi folk poetry is Dr. Viswanath Prasad's 'Magahi Sanskār-Gīt', Bihar Rashtrabhasha Parishad, Patna, 1962 (p. 308), with a short vocabulary, where we have songs and poems on social events like birth, *upanayana*, marriage and death, etc. Dr. Srimati Sampatti Āryāṇī's 'Magahī Vyākaraṇa-Kōṣa' gives a fairly comprehensive grammar of Magahi (pp. 1–86) and a vocabulary of Magahi words (pp. 1–66), published by the Hindi Sāhitya Sansār, Delhi and Patna, 1965—the grammar (in Hindi) is in the Grierson tradition, a little more extensive than Grierson's pioneer work on the language. A society for research into Magahi language and literature and Magadhan Culture has been started in January 1967—the 'Magadh Śōdh Samsthān' (Amber, Bihar Sharif, Patna District), and one number of its journal, the 'Śōdh', has so far appeared (June 1969). Volumes on the grammar and the history of literature of Magahi are being got ready for publication, together with anthologies of Magahi verse and prose and a Magahi lexicon. The medium of this research programme appears to be Hindi. Attempts are being made to obtain recognition for Magahi as a literary language from the *Sahitya Akademi* of New Delhi and also from both the Government of Bihar and the Central Government.

103, *after l.* 8, *add*: The 'Varṇa-ratnākara' has been edited and published from the Asiatic Society of Calcutta in 1940 by Suniti Kumar Chatterji and Babua Misra (Sri-Krishna Misra), with the text in Nagari characters, full grammatical introduction and general introduction in Maithili and a word-index. There are some old dramas composed in Mithila from the fifteenth century onwards, with prose conversations in Sanskrit and songs in Maithili, e.g. the 'Pārijāta-haraṇa' and the 'Rukmiṇī-pariṇaya', both ascribed to Vidyapati (see G. A. Grierson's 'Introduction to the Maithili Language of North Bihar, containing Grammar, Chrestomathy, and Vocabulary', JASB, Calcutta, 1881-82) and similar dramas with songs (as well as prose portions in some cases) in Maithili used to be performed before the Newar kings in Nepal from the seventeenth century (see Nanigopal Banerji, 'Nēpālē Bāṅglā Nāṭak', VSPdP, Calcutta, 1324 B.S.; Dr. Ramdev Jha, 'Jagajjyotir-malla-kṛta Hara-Gourī-Vivāha Naṭaka,' edited with Maithili Introduction and Notes, Laheria Sarai, Darbhanga, 1970).

103, *l.* 12: Brajabuli—This literary dialect came to be known as 'Braja-buli' in Bengal, and as ব্ৰজাৱলী « Brajāwalī » in Assam. The origin of Assamese Brajāwali was along same lines as in Bengal—it was on a basis of Maithili modified by Assamese. This artificial language also spread to Orissa, and we have one of the earliest poems in this language composed in Orissa by Rāmānanda Rāy, a contemporary of Chaitanya. See Sukumar Sen's article in the VSPdP., Bengali Year 1337, pp. 143–161, on the nature of Bengali Brajabuli, and see also his big work—'A History of Brajabuli Literature', Calcutta University, 1935.

104, *footnote*: the 'Kīrtti-latā' has been published in the Bengali character, with introduction and translation in Bengali, by Mahāmahōpādhyāya Haraprasād Śastri, in 1924 (Hṛṣīkēśa Series).

104, *l.* 12: The 'Kīrtti-latā' was edited in the Nagari characters by Bāburām Saksena from Prayag, Nagari Pracharini Sabha in 1986 V.S. (A.D. 1929), with Notes. A new edition of Haraprasad Sastri's text as revised by Suniti Kumar Chatterji was brought out in the collected Bengali works of Haraprasad Sastri ('Haraprasād-Racanāvalī'), Vol. II (pp. 238–68, Bengali Translation, pp. 269–92), as edited by S. K. Chatterji and Anil Kumar Kanjilal, Eastern Trading Co., Books and Publications, Calcutta, 1366 Bengali Year (= 1959).

106, *ll.* 21–24: the earliest specimen of connected Oriya (in a contemporary document) seems to be in the bilingual inscription (Oriya and Tamil) discovered in 1916–19 of Nṛsiṃhadeva IV (thirteenth century) from Bhubanēswar. It was very carelessly edited in the JASB for 1924, pp. 41–45, by Ganapati Sarcar Vidyaratna, who thought it belonged to *c.* A.D. 1263, but actually, as in Prof. Dinesh Chandra Sircar's edition of it, it was of the time of Vīra-Narasiṃha Deva IV, *c.* A.D. 1396. Among some of the noteworthy things in this inscription, we may mention the following: (i) the vowel « ṛ » was pronounced as « ri » and not as « ru » as in Modern Oriya: cf. the spelling « Kriṣṇa » in *l.* 3; and (ii) the word « ācāya = ācārya », which occurs here, also occurred in Old Bengali (see pp. 121–122, Introduction). The writing differentiates between the dental and cerebral « l, ḷ » sounds, and the former, which is marked with a diacritical sign below as in Modern Oriya (see under Phonology, p. 538), has been wrongly transcribed as double «ll», in the verb past tense. See 'Ārtavallabha Mahānti Memorial Lectures', First Series, 1964: 'The People, Language and Culture of Orissa' by Suniti Kumar Chatterji (published by the Orissa Sahitya Akademi, Bhubaneswar, 1966), for the Old Oriya text of this Inscription of Vira-Narasimha Deva IV, *c.* A.D. 1396, with Notes and English translation as in Prof. Dinesh Chandra Sircar's paper on it in the *Epigraphia Indica,* XXXII, No. 29, pp. 229–38 (pp. 32 ff.). Other specimens of Old Oriya are discussed in the above work (pp. 30, 31, 34, 35 ff.), including the text of the speech supposed to have been made by the founder of the Jagannātha temple at Puri, as given in the old temple chronicle of Puri, the 'Mādalā Pāñji'. (This speech has been ascribed to Ananga-Bhīma-Dēva III, *c.* A.D. 1211–1238, but internal evidence would suggest that it was made by the first builder of the present Jagannātha temple over the dilapidated foundations of an earlier temple by King Yayāti-kēśarī, viz. the great Gaṅga conqueror and emperor Ananta-varman Cōḍa-gaṅga-Dēva, A.D. 1078–1147). Although not in a contemporaneous document, the text of this speech, if it really goes back to Ananta-varman Cōḍa-gaṅga-Dēva, would be our oldest relic of continuous Old Oriya of *c.* A.D. 1100.

109, *ll.* 13–21: the 'Ṭīkā-sarvasva' was written Śaka 1082: Pandit T. Gaṇapati Śāstri published the first part in 1911, and completed the entire work in 1917.

109, *bottom of page, within square brackets at the end*: *add*: See also Niranjan Prasad Chakravarti: 'Les Mots *Bhāṣā* dans le Commentaire de Sarvānanda sur L'Amarakośa', in the 'Journal Asiatique', July-September 1926, pp. 81–100.

110, *l.* 2: *read* Caryā *for* Carjā.

110, *l.* 17: The 'Gōrakha-Bōdha'. The text of this important work, as preserved in MSS. from Rajasthan, will be found in Dr. Pītāmbar-datt Baḍthwāl's book 'Gōrakha-Bānī', Hindi Sahitya Sammelan, Prayag, 1999 V.S. Internal evidence of the text would show that there was certainly a Bengali or Early Eastern Magadhan source for the 'Gōrakha-Bōdha'; e.g. lines like the following are certainly Early Bengali (or Early Eastern Magadhan) and no other NIA speech:

« ihā̃ hī āchai, ihā̃ hī alōpa: ihā̃ hī racilai tīni tri-lōka:
āchai saṅgai rahai juwā: tā kāraṇi ananta sidhā jogeswara huwā (p. 2)
dṛṣṭi agrē dṛṣṭi lukāïbā, surati lukāïbā kānaṃ,
nāsikā agrē pawana lukāïbā, taba rahi gayā pada nirabā̃naṃ (p. 27)
āwō dēwī pa̯isō, dwādasa ā̃gula paisō:
pa̯isata pa̯isata hōi sukha, taba janama marana kā dukha (p. 53)
āpā bhāñjibā, sata-gura khōjibā jāi, joga-pantha na karibā hēlā:
phiri phiri manikhā-janama na pāïbā, hari lai sidha-purisa-sū̃ mēlā (p. 67) »

Most of the ideas and expressions belong to pan-Indian medieval Yoga, but nevertheless there are throughout certain locutions and phrases which are strongly suggestive of Old Bengali than of any other form of NIA. Some grammatical forms are of Old Bengali (or of Old Assamese, or Old Oriya), and so are many of the specific terms and words.

113, *after line* 7, *add*: The different editions of the Caryā-padas, after the *editio princeps* of Haraprasad Sastri, and studies on them:

1. Muhammad Shahidullah: 'Les Chants Mystiques de Kanha et de Saraha', Paris, 1928.
2. Prabodh Chandra Bagchi: 'Dōhākōsa': Journal of the Department of Letters, Calcutta University, Vol. XXVIII, 1935.
3. Prabodh Chandra Bagchi: 'Materials for a critical edition of the Old Bengali Caryapadas' (a Comparative study of the Text and the Tibetan translation), Part I, Journal of the Department of Letters, Calcutta University, Vol. XXX, 1938.
4. Muhammad Shahidullah: 'Buddhist Mystic Songs', Dacca University Studies, Vol. IV, No. II, 1940.
5. Manindra Mohan Basu: চর্যাপদ (in Bengali); Calcutta University, 1943; revised and enlarged second edition, Calcutta, 1964.
6. Sukumar Sen: 'Index Verborum of the Old Bengali Caryā Songs and Fragments', Indian Linguistics, Vol. IX, Calcutta, 1947.
7. Sukumar Sen: 'Old Bengali Texts, or Caryāgīti-Kōṣa', Indian Linguistics, Vol. X, Calcutta, 1948.
8. Prabodh Chandra Bagchi and Santi Bhikshu Sastri: 'Caryā-gīti-Kōṣa', Visva-Bharati University, 1956.

9. Muhammad Shahidullah: 'Caryāpadēr Pāṭh-Ālocanā', Sāhitya Patrikā, Dacca, Vol. 7, No. 2, 1370 San.

10. Saiyad Murtaza Ali: 'Caryāpader Bhāṣā', Sāhitya, Dacca, Vol. 7, No. 2, 1370 San.

11. Rahula Sankrityayana: दोहाकोष (with Hindi *chāyā*): Bihar Rāshṭra-bhāshā Parishad, Patna, 1957.

12. Rahula Sankrityayana: 'Hindi (Apabhramsa)-ke Prācīna-tama Kavi aur Kavitāēn' in his 'Purātattwa-Nibandhāvalī', Kitab-Mahal, Allahabad, 1958, pp. 131–69.

13. Atindra Majumdar: 'Caryapadas: Text, Variants, Modern Bengali Rendering, Interpretation, Glossary, Commentary, Index of Words, Bibliography' (in Bengali), Calcutta, 1961.

14. Tarapada Mukherjee: 'The Old Bengali Language and Texts', Calcutta University, 1963.

15. Sukumar Sen: 'Caryā-gīti-Padāvalī, Caryācarya-ṭīkā-Sameta' (in Bengali): Burdwan Sahitya Sabha, the Eastern Publishers, Calcutta, 1966 (the most comprehensive work on the Caryāpadas).

16. Atindra Majumdar: 'The Charyapadas' (Introduction, Text, English Translation, Notes, etc.): Calcutta, 1967.

120, *l.* 9: Lui has been described (in the introductory verse to the Sanskrit Commentary on Carya I) as 'Ādi-siddha' or 'the first Siddha' (« Śrī-Luyī-caraṇādisiddha »).

123, *footnote*: There are other passages in later Bengali literature echoing the above lines (which are proverbial in nature) from the Caryāpadas and the SKK. Thus হরিণ জগত-বৈরী আপনার মাঁসে « hariṇa jagata-bairī āpanāra mā̃sē » in the 'Caṇḍī-maṅgala Kāvya' by Kavi-Kankana Mukunda-rama Cakravarti (the late Prof. Charu Chandra Banerji of Dacca University drew our attention to this) *the stag has become the world's enemy, because of its own flesh*; বনের হরিণী আমি—কার ধার ধারি। আপনার মাংসে হৈলুঁ জগতের বৈরী « banēra hariṇī āmi—kāra dhāra dhāri; āpanāra māṃsē hailū jagatēra bairī », in the 'Harivaṁśa' by Bhavānanda (p. 234, Dacca University edition, 1932)—'*a doe living in the forest am I, I am not in the debt of any one: but because of my own flesh I have become the world's enemy;* বনের হরিণ বলে—আমি কার ধার ধারি। আপনার মাংস দিয়া জগৎ ক'রলাম বৈরী রে

« banērȧ hariṇȧ bale—āmi kār dhārȧ dhāri, āpanārȧ māṃs diyā jagat ka'rlām bairī rē » (a Sufi 'Murshidā Gān' quoted by Jasimuddin in his 'Sōjan Badiyār Ghāṭ', p. 120 (1340 B.E.): *the stag in the forest says—Who am I indebted to? (Yet) through my own flesh I have made the world my foe.* Cf. also the echo of another passage in the Caryā-padas (Caryā 8). নগর-বাহিরি রে ডোম্বি তোহোরি কুড়িয়া। ছোই ছোই জাইসি বাম্‌হণা নাডিআ।। « nagara-bāhiri rē Ḍōmbi tōhōri kuḍiā: chōi chōi jāïsi Bāmhaṇā Nāḍiā » '*O Dombi, thy hut is outside of the city, yet thou goest about, touching and touching the shaven-headed Brahman*'—as in পুখুর পাড়েতে সদা ডোমের কুড়িয়া। ঘন ঘন আইসে যায় ব্রাহ্মণ-বড়ুয়া।। « pukhurȧ pāḍētē sadā Ḍōmērȧ kuḍiyā: ghana ghana āise jāy Brāhmaṇa-baḍuā » '*the hutment of the Ḍom (girl) is away by the side of the tank, and the Brahman lad comes and goes frequently*' (quoted by Sukumar Sen in his 'Bāngȧlā Sāhityer Kathā', 3rd edition, Calcutta University, 1942, p. 82, from ধর্মপূজার ছড়া « Dharma-pūjār chaḍā » *Verses for Worship of Dharma* in the ঘরভাঙ্গা « Ghar-Bhāṅgā » *House-Breaking* sub-section of the গাজন « Gājan » *Dharma-Festival* Section.

123, *l.* 12: *add*: See *post*, p. 904, *footnote*, for a passage in Old Bengali (or Old Magahi ?) of the eleventh century, which may be corrected as « bhāla hōu, nātha-Atīśa, bhāta aṇāa, bhāta aṇāa ». In Lama Tāranātha's first book on India, 'the Mine of Precious Stones', translated into German by Grünwedel ('Edelsteinmine', Petrograd, 1914), English abstract by Bhupendranath Datta (Calcutta, Ramakrishna Vedanta Matha, 19B Raja Rajakrishna Street, 1944), we have this story (p. 26): the Siddha Jālandhari, disguised as a Hāḍī or Sweeper and remover of dead animals, came to Cāṭigrāma or Chittagong, the capital of King Gopī-candra, went to the king's fruit garden and uttered the words « nārikēla bhikasavo (= ? bhikkhawō̃) » ? *I beg for a coconut,* and the fruits of the tree came down to him, and after having drunk the coconut water, he said: « nārikēla, upara jāhi » *coconuts, go up,* and the fruits went back to the top of the tree as before.

127, *after l.* 2: *add*:

In the Sikh 'Guru-granth', or 'Granth Sāhib' compiled by Guru Arjun in A.D. 1604, there are two hymns in a mixed Apabhramsa and Old Hindi Speech (under Rāg Mārū and Rāg Gūjarī), which have been discussed by me in my Bengali article on Jayadeva published in the 'Bhārata-varsha' for Śrāvaṇa 1350: English translation in the Dr. S. H. Dhruva Commemoration Volume, Part III, pp. 183–96, Gujarāt Vidyā-sabhā, Ahmedabad, 1946.

I have given the texts of these two with a Bengali translation and commentary (the Bengali article has been reprinted in my 'Sāṁskṛitikī', Vol. II, Calcutta, Bengali Year 1372 = 1965, pp. 58–81). The language is not Bengali. (One of these two poems ascribed to Jayadeva in the 'Guru Granth', that under Rāg Gūjarī, was translated into German and commented upon by J. Trumpp in the 'Sitzungsberichte der Königl. bayer. Akademie der Wissenschaften, Philosophisch-philologische Classe', 7, January 1879, in his paper 'Die altesten Hinduī-Gedichte', pp. 1–48).

127, *after line* 2, *add*:

65a. The Sanskrit encyclopaedia 'Mānasōllāsa' or 'Abhilaṣitārtha-cintāmaṇi' (of which the first volume has been published in the Gaekwad's Oriental Series, 1925), composed in Śaka 1051 (1129 A.C.) under the auspices of King Someśvara III Bhūlōka-malla of the later Cālukya dynasty of Mahārāṣṭra, who ruled from 1127 to 1138 A.C., seems to contain a few Old Bengali lines. (Sakhāram Gaṇeś Deuskar in the Bengali Journal 'Āryāvartta' for Māgha, 1317, pp. 678–79; R. G. Bhāṇḍārkar, 'Early History of the Deccan', Bombay, 1895, pp. 89–90: Deuskar mentions a Marathi article by V. K. Rājawāḍe on this work read before the first Mahārāṣṭra Sāhitya Sammēlan which I have not seen. (I am indebted to my friend and colleague the late Professor Kshitish Chandra Chatterji, for bringing Deuskar's article to my notice).

In the section on Poetry and Music ('Gīta-Vinōda') in this work, short poems and verses in Sanskrit, Prakrit, Apabhraṁśa, 'Lāṭī', and in the Dravidian Kannaḍa speech have been given; and besides, a few verses occur, which are undoubtedly in the various NIA speeches—Old Marathi, Old Braj-bhakha and Old Bengali, to judge from at least some of the forms. The work is preserved in various MSS. at Poona, Tanjore, Bikaner and elsewhere. I could consult one of the Poona MSS. (copied Saṃvat 1930 = 1874) which happened to be in the Indian Museum in Calcutta in 1923, and through the kind offices of my friend, Sri Sris

Chandra Chatterji, Engineer and Architect, lately in the service of the Bikaner State, I also obtained (December 1923) transcripts of the relevant parts from an old MS. of the work (dated Śaka 1593 = 1671 A.C.) in the Fort Library of Bikaner. Both the MSS. are very corrupt, and although there is a close agreement between them (both seemingly being based on the same original), the bad readings make it almost impossible to restore the text of the non-Sanskrit portions from these only. Instead of attempting to give a critical edition of these portions in question, I give below tentative readings of some of the NIA passages based on a comparison of the two MSS., wherever they can be made out with any degree of certainty. We have thus—

«.. chāṃḍu chāṃḍu maī jāivō (= jāibō ? jaiba ?) Gōvinda-saha khēlaṇa ... Nārāyaṇu jagaha-kēru (-kēra) gōsāṃvī» (Bikaner, fol. 141a; Poona, fol. 168b) = *Leave (me), leave (me), I shall go to sport with Govinda ... Narayana the lord of the world.*

Bikaner fol. 141b and 142a and Poona fol. 169a, b give a song praising the ten Avatāras of Viṣṇu, which seems to represent more than one form of NIA. The first verse is in Old Marathi, and runs thus: «jēṇē rasātala-uṇu matsya-rūpēṃ vēda āṇiyalē(ṃ) ... tō saṃsāra-sāyara-tāraṇu, maha-tē(ṃ) rākhō Nārāyaṇu» *by Whom the Vedas were brought from Rasātala in the form of a fish ... the Saviour in the ocean of transmigration ... He, Nārāyana, (may) protect me.* The next verse (on the Tortoise Incarnation) is very corrupt. The third verse is as follows: «jō suvara-rūvēṃ pāyalu paīsi dāṇaü Hariṇa-kachapu mācaviṃ(?), dāḍha Gōvinda dharaṇi uddhariaṃ sō dēu ...» *Who in the form of a boar entered Pātāla and killed the demon Hiraṇya-kaśipu, Gōvinda who rescued Earth with his tusk, that God ...* This verse has Śaurasēnī affinities, as also the next two verses on Nṛsiṃha and Vāmana Avatāras, but both are hopelessly corrupt.

The sixth shows some distinctive Bengali features: « jē brāhmaṇēra-kulē(ṃ) upajiyā(ṃ), Kātavī(r)ya jēṇē bāhu-pharasē khāṇḍiyā: Paraśa-rāmu dē(v)u sē māhara (mōhara ?) maṅgala karaü» *Who was born in the family of a Brahman, by Whom with the touch of his arm Kārttavīrya was cut down, He, the God Paraśurāma, may work my welfare.* The above reading is substantially that of the Bikaner MS., and the Bengali character of this passage is shown by the pronoun « jē », and « -ē(ṃ), -ēra » affixes for the locative and genitive; and « -iyā » would be the non-l passive participle adjective (> verb past) which featured in Old Bengali (see pp. 946 ff.).

The verse describing Rāma is missing in both the MSS. That on Kṛṣṇa is apparently in Old Braj-bhakha: « Nanda-gōula jāyau̯ Kānhu jō gōvī-jaṇe(ṃ) pajihe . . . », but it is corrupt. The verse on Buddha runs thus: « Buddha-rūpēṁ jo dāṇava-surā vañcauni vēde-dūsaṇa bōl-laüṇi māyā mōhiyā, tō dēu mājhi pasāü karu » *Who in the form of Buddha, after having cheated Gods and Demons and having said words of scorn for the Vedas, led (them) astray by his Māyā—that God may grant grace to me.* It is distinctly Old Marathi. The last verse on Kalki is in Sanskrit.

The 'Mānasōllāsa has been edited by Gajanan K. Shrigondekar, (Baroda, Gaekwad's Oriental Series: Vol. I, No. XXVIII, 1925; Vol. II, No. LXXXIV, 1939; and Vol. III, No. 138, 1961). The above verses in NIA speeches will be found in Vol. III, pp. 37, 38 and 39. In the section on 'Gīta-vinōda' in this work (pp. 1–83, Vol. III), there is a mass of interesting information on Music and Singing of all sorts as known in Western India in the twelfth century. Thus, e.g. *Caryā* as a kind of poetry with a spiritual meaning as used by the Yogis has been mentioned (see *op. cit.* pp. 47, 60, 64 and 81, the same statement being repeated more than once: e.g. « ādhyātmikārtha-yuktāni caryā-nāmni praban-dhakē », and « kathāsu ṣaṭpadī yōjyā, vivāhē dhavalas tathā : utsavē maṅgalō gēyaś, caryā Yōgi-janais tathā »; and four lines in a Prakrit speech, very corrupt in the MSS., have been given twice as a specimen of a Caryā song). The relevant passages in the 'Mānasōllāsa' have been already noted with comments by Dr. Sukumar Sen in his comprehensive 'History of Bengali Literature', in Bengali, Vol. I, First Half, 5th edition, pp. 62-63 (published by the Eastern Publishers, Calcutta, 1970).

127, *l.* 10. *Correct to*: and Śrī-Kara Nandi's 'Mahābhārata-Aśvamēdha-parvan'.

129, *l.* 11: It must be said that Professor Sukumar Sen is skeptical about the fifteenth century being the date of 'Śrī-kṛṣṇa-kīrttana'—he is in favour of bringing it down to the sixteenth century, and even later. See his 'History of Bengali Literature' in Bengali, Vol. I, part I, 3rd edition, Eastern Publishers, Calcutta 6, 1959, pp. 127–33.

131, *ll.* 27 *ff.* Ḍāk the Gōwālā (cowherd) is also well known in Bihar as a sage and author of proverbial sayings, as Sir George Grierson told me. See also Mm. Haraprasād Śāstrī on Ḍāk and Khanā in the Bengali journal 'Prācī' (Dacca) for Śrāvaṇa, 1330 Bengali Era (reprinted in the first volume of 'Haraprasād-Racanāvalī', pp. 308–14).

132, *l.* 24: *Correct to* Śrī-kara Nandī.

136, *l.* 30: The 'Crepar Xaxtrer Orthbhed' has been reprinted (with grammatical Introduction by Suniti Kumar Chatterji) in the original Roman script with transcription in Bengali characters by Sajani Kanta Das, Calcutta, 1346 B.S./A.D. 1939. The 'Brāhmaṇ-Rōmān Kātholik Saṁvād', an earlier work in Bengali under Portuguese inspiration, preserved in manuscript at Coimbra, Portugal, has been edited and published by the University of Calcutta by Prof. Surendra Nath Sen in 1937.

137, *l.* 13: *read* form *for* from.

143, *ll.* 4, 5: The special treatment of the aspirate « h » and the voiced aspirated stops, nasals and liquids « gh, jh, ḍh, dh, bh; ḍh-ṛh : rh, lh; nh, mh » is something peculiar to East Bengali, and this phenomenon I found out some years after the publication of the ODBL in 1926. The aspirate « h » is changed into glottal stop « ʔ », and the other aspirated sounds have the glottal stop replacing the aspirate « h », with high tone on the syllable. There are a number of accompanying phonetic modifications (see Suniti Kumar Chatterji—'Recursives in New Indo-Aryan' in the *Indian Linguistics*, Vol. I, Pt. I, 1931, pp. 15–44; 'Mahāprāṇa Varṇa', pp. 199–222 in 'Bāṅgālā Bhāṣā-tattwer Bhūmikā', Calcutta University, 1942 (and subsequent editions); 'Indo-Aryan and Hindi', 2nd edition, Calcutta, 1960, pp. 111–16, also pp. 322–24 (reprinted 1970); 'Glottal Spirants and the Glottal Stop in the Aspirates in New Indo-Aryan', pp. 407–14, in 'In Honour of Daniel Jones', Longmans, London, 1964). A full study of the behaviour of the aspirate and of the aspirated stops will be of paramount importance for Indo-Aryan phonetics and phonology. As already noted by myself and others, there appears to be some connexion between the treatment of the voiced aspirates and the aspirate in some East Bengali dialects on the one hand and speeches of North-western and Western India like Hindki (Lahnda or West Panjabi), Eastern Panjabi, Dogri, Rajasthani and Gujarati, as well as Sindhi, on the other.

144, *after l.* 11 *add*: Maimansingh and Barisal dialects also change « p » to « ꜰ, or ϕ » (or « pꜰ, or pϕ » ?).

144, *l.* 19: In the Barisal district, we have also চলিয়া « caliyā » *having gone* > « tsɔlyā < tsɔlgyā », পড়িয়া « paṛiyā » *having fallen* > « ꜰɔrgyā ».

147, *l.* 10: In these dialects, we have also the Early Bengali affix for the future, first person, « -ibō̃ », changed to « -imu, -mu » and the original present particle affix « -it- » is also used as a future base, in negative statements.

148, *l.* 30: *read* « bhāṣā » *for* « bhasā ».

156, *l.* 13: *read* vēlā *for* vēla; *l.* 15, *correct to* between.

157, *l.* 13: *read* « nī̃b » *for* « nīb »; *l.* 14, *read* tāmra *for* tamra.

159, *ll.* 14, 15: Pischel gives ('Grammatik der Prakrit-sprachen', § 304) « uṭṭa, iṭṭa » as MIA forms. The deaspiration in these words thus goes back to MIA times, and the W. Hindi « ū̃ṭ, ī̃ṭ » are obviously based on MIA « *uṇṭa, *iṇṭa » showing spontaneous nasalization (discussed at pp. 368 ff.).

166, *l.* 6: *after* mī̃ *read* myā̃.

167, *l.* 19: But it is to be noted that some of the commonest words differ in Marathi from most of the other NIA languages: e.g. « ḍoḷ » *eye* (found in Oriya), « pāhṇē̃ » *to see*, « aikṇē̃ » *to hear*, « tup » *ghee*, « wāran » *pulses*, « bhākrā » *bread*, « muḷgā, muḷī » *boy, girl*, « ghētṇē̃ » *to take*, « bāykō » *a woman*, etc.

170, *l.* 5 *from bottom of page*: *after* Dravidian sounds, and *add*: these (barring the last, which is found in Dravidian—in Tamil only, to be precise).

176, *l.* 7: *read* « ghōṛā-ṭōṛā » *for* « ghōrā-ṭōṛā ».

176, *l.* 11: *read* « kudure-gidure » *for* « kudire-gidire ».

176, 'Echo Words', or 'Jingles':

l. 14, *correct* « dat-bat » to « dat-pat ». *Add, in this line*: Other Sinhalese examples are « karatta-baratta » *carts, etc.*, « peṭṭi-beṭṭi » *boxes, etc.*, « harak-barak » *cows, etc.*, « kuḍa-buḍa » *umbrellas, etc.*, « sereppu-bereppu » *shoes, etc.*, « paḍikkam-ba° » *spittoons, etc.*, « patra-ba° » *newspapers, etc.*, « kæti-bæti » *knives, etc.*, « watura-ba° » *water, etc.*

176, *l.* 16: Some Bengali dialects (East Bengali—Dacca, Sylhet and Tipperah districts) take also « -u- » besides « -ṭ- »—this is possibly due to dialectal miscegenation (with North Indian Awadhi, Hindustani and other speeches).

'Echo Words' are found in languages outside India: e.g. Japanese, where it is called *Nigori*, i.e. voicing of the initial consonant of the word, e.g. « tokoro » *place*, « tokoro-dokoro » *places, etc., all sorts of places*; « shina » *object*, « shina-jina » *objects of all kinds*; « kuni, kuni-guni » *various countries*; « kusuri, kusuri-gusuri » *medicines of all kinds*; in Turkish dialects, where the consonant substituted for the initial consonant of the original word is « -m- ». It is also found in Modern Persian, either as a substratum from the pre-Aryan speeches of Iran, or through Turanian, i.e. Turki influence: e.g. « lūtī-pūtī » *vagabond, etc.*, « kafš-pafš » *shoes, etc.*, « xirt-pirt » *small articles*; « duzd-puzd » *thieves, etc.*, « šutar-mutar » *camels, etc.*, « qatir-matir » *mules, etc.*; « cilau-milau » *rice-dish, etc.*, « gūšt-mūšt » *meat, etc.*, « farš-marš » *covering or cloth, etc.* There is at times introduction of this habit into French by Turkish speakers: e.g. *c'était une grande affaire: il y avait beaucoup de monde là, des* princes-minces, *des* ducs-mucs, *des* barons-marons *et des autres personnalités.*

We have also these Echo Words in Verbal Forms and Particles: e.g. Bengali দেখ্‌বে-টেখ্‌বে « dekhbe-ṭekhbe » *you will see and watch, will look after*; বলা-টলা চ'ল্‌বে না « balā-ṭalā ca'lbe nā » *it won't do to speak out*; কাঁদ্‌লে-টাঁদ্‌লে « kā̃dle-ṭā̃dle » *wept and worried*; « nā-ṭā śunbō nā » *I won't hear any denial*—lit. *no or naught*, etc. See S. K. Chatterji—Higher Bengali Grammar in Bengali ('Saralā Bhāṣā-Prakāśā Bāṅgālā Vyākaraṇā') under 'Reduplicated Words and Echo Words', Revised Edition, 1971, pp. 223–32.

177, *ll.* 21 *ff.*: This idiomatic use of a verbal conjunctive meaning *having said* is a common idiom in Tibeto-Burman as well—in Kuki-Chin, for instance —and it is also found in Burmese (see LSI, III, Part III, p. 5); and it is common in Bodo also, which was the original language of a large section of present-day Bengali-speakers in North and East Bengal (J. D. Anderson in the JRAS, 1913, pp. 867 ff.).

178, *add to the list of references, at the end of para* **83**: Suniti Kumar Chatterji, 'Two New Indo-Aryan Etymologies (cāul, √puṛ)' in the 'Zeitschrift für Indologie', Leipzig, 1932; 'Non-Aryan Elements in Indo-Aryan' in the 'Journal of the Greater India Society', Calcutta, Vol. III, 1936, pp. 43 ff.; 'Some Etymological Notes', in the 'New Indian Antiquary' publication—'A Volume of Indian and Iranian Studies presented to Sir E. Denison Ross', 1939, pp. 68–74; J. Burrow, 'Non-Aryan Influence on Sanskrit': Chapter VIII of 'The Sanskrit Language', London, 1956, with word lists; A. N. Upadhye, 'Kanarese Words in Desi Lexicons', Annals BhRI, Poona 1931, Vol. XII, iii, pp. 274–84 (39 words); Thirumala Ramachandra, 'Some Telugu Words in the Gāthāsaptaśatī', 26th International Congress of Orientalists, New Delhi, 1964, pp. 1–20.

179 *ff.*, *Appendix C*: Additional Names of Places and Persons from Old Bengal Inscriptions.

179, *after Section* 84, *add*: Susunia Rock Inscriptions of Chandra-varman (*c.* A.D. 340–60); « Puṣkaraṇā = Pokharnā », village in Bankura District, cf. Suniti Kumar Chatterji, article in the 'Vaṅga-śrī' (Bengali Monthly), Phālguna, 1339 Bengali Year, pp. 135-36: 'Prācīna Vaṅgēr Puṣkaraṇā-janapada'.

179, *l.* 7: *from bottom*: *add, within square brackets*: In NB also we have the word ডুঙ্গরী « ḍungȧri » meaning *hillock*, as in ফুল-ডুঙ্গরী « phulȧ-ḍuṅgȧrī » *Flower-Hill* near Ghatsila in the Dhalbhum area, beside টিকর, টিকুরি « ṭikarȧ, ṭikuri » which also means *high land* and is found in place-names, like শাঁখ-টিকর « śā̃khȧ-ṭikarȧ » *Conchshell-hillock* (this has been through mistake transformed into শক্তিগড় « Śakti-gaṛhȧ », and সরাই-টিকর Sarāi-Ṭikarȧ » *Hillock of the Inn*, which are places near Burdwan Town, as well as গঙ্গাটিকুরি « Gaṅgā-Ṭikuri » and বালটিকরী « Bālȧ-Ṭikȧrī » which are other place-names in Bengal).

179, *last line but one*: *Correct date to* 543–44 A.C.

180, *after l.* 2, *add*:

(2A) Kalāikuri-Sultānpur Copper Plate Inscription of Gupta Year 120 = A.D. 439 (Rajshahi District): Dinesh Chandra Sircar, 'Select Inscriptions', Vol. I, 2nd edition, 1965, pp. 352 ff.:

« Śṛṅgavēra-vīthi » = modern *Siṅgrā* (?) ; « Pūrṇa-kausikā ; Hasti-śīrṣa ; Vibhītakī ; Gulma-gandhikā ; Dhānya-pāṭalikā; Saṁgōhālī ; Vāṭānadī (= modern *Bara-naī*) ; Tāpasa-pottaka ; Dayitā-pottaka ; Citra-vātaṅgaraa ».

(2B) Bāigrām Copper-plate Inscription, Gupta Year 128 (= A.D. 448): Bogra (Baguṛā) District. Dinesh Chandra Sircar, 'Select Inscriptions', pp. 355 ff.

« Pañca-nagarī (= modern *Pānc-bibi*, name Muhammadanized for a possible change of MIA *pañca-naarī to *pañca-nārī *Five Women*); Kulavṛddhi, Vāyi-grāma (= modern *Bāi-grām*), Śrī-gōhāli, Trivṛtā ».

(2C) Pāhāṛpur Copper-plate Inscription, Gupta Year 159 (= A.D. 479), Rajshahi District: Dinesh Chandra Sircar, 'Select Inscriptions', pp. 359 ff.

« Dakṣiṇāṁśaka-vīthi; Nāgiraṭṭa-maṇḍala, Palāśātta, Vaṭagōhāli-Jambudēva; Pṛṣṭhima-pottaka; Goṣāṭa-puñjaka; Nitra-gōhālī; Pañca-stūpa (= modern Pā̃c-thupī, elsewhere).

(2D) Faridpur Copper-plate of the time of Gopa-Candra (*c.* middle of the sixth century A.D.): Faridpur District, Dinesh Chandra Sircar, 'Select Inscriptions', pp. 370 ff.

« Vāraka (< vāruka)-maṇḍala; Navyāvakāśikā; Dhruvilāṭī agra-hāra; Karaṅga; Śīla-kuṇḍa-grāma ».

(2E) Guṇāi-ghar grant of the time of Vainya-Gupta: Gupta Year 188 = 507 A.C. (Comilla, Tippera District): Dinesh Chandra Bhatta-charyya, 'Indian Historical Quarterly', Vol. 6, No. 1, March 1930, pp. 45–60; also 'Pravāsī', Bhādra 1338, pp. 673 ff.; Dinesh Chandra Sircar, 'Select Inscriptions', pp. 340 ff.

The words « Khāṭa, Jōlaka, Nauyōga, Hajjikā » and « Vilāla » occur in this inscription for certain natural features: « Khāṭa » = modern NB খাড়ী « khāṛī » ; « Jōlaka » = NB জোল « jōla » and জুলি « juli » *channel*; « Hajjikā », cf. NB হাজা « hājā » as in হাজা নদী « hājā-nadī » = *dried up river*; and probably « *Vilāla* » is connected with the word বিল « bila » meaning *a marsh or a marshy lake;* and « Nau-yōga » would appear to mean *a gathering place for boats.* The following place-names occur in this inscription according to the later readings given in the

'Pravāsī' article: « Naḍadādaka Grāma; Kantē-dādaka Grāma; Guṇēka-grahāra Grāma » also « Guṇika-grahāra (cf. NB Guṇāighara village); Gaṇēśvara-Vilāla Puṣkariṇī; Surinasira Purṇṇēka-Kṣētra; Dēsi-bhōga Puṣkariṇī; Kampiyakāditya-Bandhu-Kṣētrāṇām Sīmā; Pakka-Villāla-Kṣētra; Nakhardda-cārika-Kṣetra; Jōlari-Kṣētra; Nāgī-jōḍāka-Kṣetra; Buddhāka-Kṣētra; Kālāka-Kṣētra; Khaṇḍa-Viḍuggurika-Kṣētra; Maṇi-bhadra-Kṣētra; Yajña-rāta-Kṣetra; Pradamara-Nauyōga-Khāṭa; Cūḍā-maṇi-Nagaraśrī-Nauyōga-Śākya-Bhikṣvācāryya-Jitasēna-Vaihārika-Kṣētra; Pradyumnēśvara-Dēvakula-Kṣētra; Cāṭa-Gāṅga; Daṇḍa-Puṣkiṇī = Puṣkariṇī ». There is a mention of « Karaṇa-Kāyastha », i.e. Kayastha *clerk*; and the expression is noteworthy —« Khaṇḍa-phuṭṭa-pratisaṁskāra-karaṇāya », i.e. *to make repairs of breakage and leakage.*

(2F) Mallasārul Copper-plate Grant of Gōpa or Gōpacandra and Vijaya-Sēna, in Burdwan district, *c.* A.D. 550, VSPdP 44, No. 1, pp. 17–21—Nani Gopal Majumdar; also 'Calcutta Review', March 1938—Sukumar Sen; and 'Select Inscriptions', Vol. I, 2nd edition, University of Calcutta, 1965, pp. 372 ff., by Dinesh Chandra Sircar.

« Vardhamāna Bhukti: village Bakkattāka (= NB বাকতা Bākatā); Nirvṛta-Vāṭaka; Ardha-kāraka (= NB আদরা Ādarā); Kapistha-Vāṭaka (NB কৈতর Kaitar); Vaṭa-ballāka; Koddavīra; Gōdhā-Grāma (= Gōha-gāṃva, NB গোগাঁ Gōgā̃; also Sōha-Grāma); Śālmali-Vāṭaka (= modern Bengali শিমুল-ডাঙ্গা Śimula-ḍāṅgā); Madhu-Vāṭaka (= NB মহুড়া, মহড়া, মওড়া Mahuḍā, Mahaṛā, Maoṛā); Khaṇḍa-Jōṭikā (from Khaṇḍa-Jōtikēya); Vindhya-Pura (from Vindhya-Purēya); Vetra-Getta; Amrāgarttikā ».

(2G) Two copper-plates of Śaśāṅka (*c.* A.D. 600–625), Regnal Year 19: Dinesh Chandra Sircar in the 'Pravāsī', Śrāvana 1350, pp. 291–300: cf. also 'Mādhavī' for Āṣāḍha 1345, pp. 3–6, by Manishinath Roy.

« Tavīra » = *District Office.*

« Kētaka-Padra; Kumbhāra-Padraka » villages (the second = NB কুমারপাড়া « Kumāra-pāṛā »).

(2H) Mahīpāla-Dēva's Nārāyaṇapura Grant, at the base of a Gaṇēśa image, near Chandpur in Comilla district:

« Bilikandhaka » village, in Samataṭa district (= village বিল-কেন্দুয়া, « Bil-kēnduā » near Bāghāuṛā, Dist. Tipperah).

180, *after l.* 14, *add*:

In connexion with the above is to be taken (iv) the Ghugrāhāṭi Copper-plate of Samācāra-dēva (cf. Ep. Ind., 1925, Vol. XVIII, pp. 134, 74 ff., edited by Nalini-Kanta Bhaṭṭaśālī, M.A.), which mentions « Navyāvakāsikā », as well as « Vāraka-maṇḍala », and « Vyāghra-cōraka » and « Gōpēndra-cōraka » village, and « Vidyādhara-jōṭikā » ; and among personal names it gives « Pavittruka, Dāmuka, Vatsa-kuṇḍa, Śuci-pālita, Vihita-ghōṣa, Śūra-datta, Priya-datta, Janārddana-kuṇḍa ».

Para 87: This Copper-plate Inscription has been edited and published by Dr. L. D. Barnett in the Ep. Ind. ('Vappaghōshavāṭa Grant of Jayanāga', Vol. XVIII, pp. 60 ff.).

182, *l.* 24: « koppam »: Compare also Tamil « kuppam » *village*.

183, *After l.* 16, *add*:

(11A) Copper-plate Grant of Gopāla-deva II (*c.* 940–970 A.C.), discovered in Maldah district: Kshitish Chandra Varman, 'Bhārata-varṣa' for Caitra 1343, XXIV, II, 4, pp. 638–43: village « Ānanda-pura » (an *Agrahāra*), within « Kuddāla-khāta Viṣaya » or district in Puṇḍravardhana Bhukti; « Vaṭa-parbhata-samarasita (= °parvata-samāśrita) Śrīmaj-jayaskandhāvāra » *the king's camp established on Baniyan-tree Hill*; « Kāśyapa-gōtrīya-Yājñika-Śrīdhara-Śarmā » from « Sīha-grāma » *Lion village*; village « Mukata-vāstu »; Engraver « Vimala-dāsa, the son of Madya-dāsa ».

183, *after l.* 29, *add*:

(14A) Dhulla Copper-plate of Śrī-candra: « Dūrvvā-pattra » village in « Vallī-muṇḍa-Maṇḍala (in Khaḍira-vallī-Viṣaya) »; « Loṇia-jōḍa-prastara » = *salty water-channel rock*; « Tivara-villi » village = *the Beel or marshy lake of the Tīvara people*; « Parkaḍi-muṇḍa » village = *the head of the Parkaṭī or Pākuṛ tree*; « Yola-Maṇḍala (Yōla = Jōla) »: *water-channel district*; « Ikuaḍa-Viṣaya »; « Mūla-patra » village.

(14B) Edilpur Grant of Śri-Candra: Village « Lēliya (in Kumāra-talaka Maṇḍala) » in « Sataṭa-padmāvatī-Viṣaya » *the district of Padmāvati along with the river-bank*.

186, *l.* 31: *Correct* Five *to* Seven.

187, *l.* 10: The Govindapur Grant has since been edited by Prof. A. C. Vidyabhushana in the 'Bhārata-varṣa' for Phālguna, 1332.

187, *after last line in this page, add*:

(vi) Bhāwāl Grant (Nalini-Kānta Bhaṭṭaśālī 'The Lost Bhowal Copper-plate of Lakshmaṇa-Sēna Dēva of Bengal', IHQ, Vol. 3, 1927, No. I, pp. 89–96);

(vii) Saktipur-Kāndi Grant (Ramesh Basu, VSPdP, Vol. 37, pt. IV, pp. 216 ff.) «Kaṅka-grāma Bhukti» area attached to «Kumbhi-nagara in Kumāra-pura Caturaka (or *Circle*); Bāṛaha-kōṇa (= *12-corner*); Vallihiṭa Nijha; Rāghava-haṭṭa; Mōcā Nadi (= *Plantain-flower River*? cf. N.B. «mōcā» মোচা); Acchama-Gōpatha; Māli-kuṇḍa (= *Gardener's Spring*?); Bhagaḍi-Khaṇḍa-Ksētra (in Vāsa-sthalī); Madhugiri-Maṇḍala»: villages «Tāmara-vaḍā» and «Vijahara-pura»; «Parajāna-Gōpatha» *Cattle-track of the Tenants*?; and the Water-channels, «Lāṇgala-jōli, Sca-prabaddha-jōli(?), Cākaliyā-jōli».

188, *after l.* 5, *add*:

(27A) Sahitya Parishad (Calcutta) Copper-plate of Viśvarūpa-sēna, found in Central Dacca, from Susang Raj family: «Tyastana-dēvī(?), Rāma-siddhi-pāṭaka», village in Navya region within the Vaṅga district of Puṇḍra-vardhana-Bhukti; «Vinayatilaka» village; «Ājikula-pāṭaka» in «Nava-saṃgraha-Caturaka» in «Madhu-kṣīraka-avṛtti(?)»; village «Dēula-hasti» in «Lauhaṇḍa Caturaka» within «Vikramapura»; «Ghaghara-katti-pāṭaka» in «Vikramapura Caturaka»; «Pātila-Dīvikā» (= *Earthen-pot Island*?, N.B. পাতিল «pātila» = *thin earthen-ware pot for cooking*); and «Dībikā = Dvīpikā»; «Vaṅgāla-vaḍā; Jayajahaḍa».

188, *l.* 11: *add after* Viśva-rūpa-sēna:

«Madana-pāḍā» in Kōṭālipāṛā parganā, district Faridpur.

188, *after l.* 20, *add at the end*:

(29A) Ādābāḍi Copper-plate of Daśaratha-dēva: N. G. Majumdar in 'Inscriptions of Bengal', Vol. III, 1929, pp. 181–82; also Nalini-Kanta Bhaṭṭaśāli in the 'Bhārata-varṣa', Pauṣa, 1332 B.S., pp. 78–81: end of the thirteenth century.

The following গাঁঞি «gāñi» or village-names of Brahman donees occur in this inscription: «diṇḍī; pālī; sēv, sēū; māsacaṭaka (māsacaḍaka);

mūla; sēhaṇḍāyī; puti; mahāntiyāḍā; karañja-grāmī ». Besides, the following localities are also mentioned: « antarvvāṭī » (= modern « Ādābāḍī »); « bāndikhāṇḍā » (= modern « bainkhāḍā »); navasaṁkhaha; vīṣayipāḍā; nayanāva; mūladāva; vaḍāilā; bhāṅganiyā; gaṇāgrāma; māntahaṭā ».

188, *at the end, add*:

110A. For a similar occurrence of non-Aryan elements in place-names in inscriptions from early Orissa, see 'Artavallabha Mahanti Memorial Lectures (First Series, 1964): The People, Language and Culture of Orissa' by Suniti Kumar Chatterji, Orissa Sahitya Akademi, Bhubaneswar, 1966, pp. 21–22.

195, *after l.* 6 *add*: (আ)সওয়ার « (ā)sawāra » *horseman, trooper,* সওয়ারি « sawāri » *rider (on horse, in carriage)*: the word occurs in the Bharhut and Sanchi inscriptions as « asavāri », from Old Persian « asa-bāri » *horseman* (= New Persian « suwar »); গোঁড়া « gōṛā » *supporter, loyal supporter, orthodox follower, unreasoning partisan* = গুণ্ডা « guṇḍā » *a hired rough, a ruffian, a hooligan*: Modern Persian « gund » *crowd, collected people,* Pahlavi « gund » *army,* Arabicized to جند « jund » = Sanskrit « vṛnda » *row, group, company.*

195, *after l.* 18, *add*: কোণ « koṇa » *corner,* from MIA and Skt. = Greek « gōnos »; কঁ্যাদরা, কেঁদরা « kǣdərā < kènda-rā » *centre,* used in Astrology, e.g. কঁ্যাদরায় শনি « kèndərāy Śani » = *Saturn in the centre,* from « kendra » *centre, tbh.* « kēda, kenda- + ṭa > -ḍa > -ṛa + -ā » affixes: Greek « kentron » = *centre.*

196, *ll.* 10, 20, 22: More Gujarati and Marathi words—তকলী « takəlī « *spindle,* Gujarati, for pure Bengali টাকুয়া, টাউক্যা, টেকো « ṭākuā, ṭāukyā, ṭēkō » from Sanskrit « takru-»; Marathi চৌথ « cauth » *one-fourth of the revenue of a state*; পিণ্ডারী « piṇḍārī » from « peṇḍhārī » *a freebooter, an armed robber.*

196, *last line but one*: *read* « śuruṭṭu » *for* « suḷuṭṭu ».

197, *l.* 1: *after* Tibetan « blama », *add* টাঙ্গন « ṭāṅgan » *a hill pony, Bhotia pony* = Tibetan « rta-ŋāŋ ».

197, *l.* 5: *add*: Some recent loans from South Indian languages, mainly Tamil: the names of certain South Indian dishes—ইড়লী « iḍlī » *steamed cake of mixed rice and pulse paste,* ধোসা « dhōsā » *powdered rice and pulse fried pancake,* উপ্‌মা « upmā » *a salted pudding of semolina or cream of wheat, or rice, fried in ghee or oil,* সাম্বর « sāmbar » *lentils with tamarind and vegetables like 'drum sticks',* রসম্ « rasam » *soup of dāl with chillies and tamarind, 'Mulligatawny Soup'.*

198, 199: The word « dhītā » (as the source of « jhī ») has also been derived from the Indo-European « *√dhē » *suck* (= OIA « dhā »), which we find in the Latin « fī-lius ».

202, *l.* 30, *after* last quarter of the sixteenth century, *add*: The earliest inscriptions of the Turki conquerors of Bihar and Bengal were in Arabic, the sacred language of Islam, and not in Persian: e.g. the inscriptions in Bengal of Ulugh-i-'Azam Ẓafar Khān Bahrām Itagīn, who conquered Sātgāon (Saptagrāma), *c.* 1298, and settled down there; and his mosque at Gangārāmpur (Gaur), and at Tribeni near Sātgāon have Arabic inscriptions.

203, *l.* 22: *read* fatḫ *for* faṭḫ.

204, *footnote*: About the number of Persian words in the 'Śrīkṛṣṇa-kīrttana': Professor Sukumar Sen, on closer investigation, thinks the number is much higher—17, in fact (in a personal communication). This has to be looked into, but the number certainly would come up to at least 10.

206, *after line* 25, *add*:

Some slight influence of Persian syntax is noticeable on Bengali, particularly in the use of the pronominal particle কি « ki » to introduce a dependent clause (this is found in Hindustani also): e.g. Common Colloquial Standard Bengali সে ব'ল্লে কি . . . « se ba'lålē ki (bollē ki) » *he said that. . .* = Persian « ān guft kih. . . » (Pure Bengali or Early Bengali would be সে বলিল যে. . . « sē balila jē. . . »; and an expression like বলো দেখি « balô dēkhi » *do tell me,* literally '*tell me, I see*': cf. Persian « ba-gō, bih-binam » *say, I may see* = *do tell me*; মন যা চায় তাই করে « manå jā cāy tāi karē » *he does what pleases his mind:* cf. Persian « harkih har-cih bi-kunad, dil bi-xvāh ast ». Certain idioms were taken over from or reinforced by Persian: e.g. মাথা বাঁচানো « māthā bā̃cānō » *to save one's head* = *to evade* = « sar dar kardan »; কপালে লেখা আছে « kapālē lēkhā āchē » *it is written on the forehead* = *it is destined,* cf. Persian « dar pīšānī-e-man ham-cū nūštah šudah ast ki. . . »; the old-fashioned expression গু খেয়েছি «gu khēyēchi» *I have eaten dirt = I have told a lie* = «gūh xūrdah būdam»; etc.

213, *last line in footnote* 1, *read* «khājānci» for «khajañcī».

215, *l.* 6: *Correct* 10 *to* 30.

l. 18: The common Bengali slang expression মেটে ফিরিঙ্গি «mēṭē phiriṅgi» *a half-caste, a Eurasian, a mixed European, a coloured or dark-skinned Eurasian*, suggests the word মাটি > মেটে «māṭi = māṭiyā, mēṭē» *from the soil*; but it is probably the French word «métis» *a mixed breed, a Mestizo*, and this French word may also have given another word for a Eurasian; টেঁশ, ট্যাঁশ «ṭēś, ṭyāś».

215, *l.* 22: *read* ইস্ক্রুপ্ *for* ইস্ক্রপ.

223: *add, at the end*: See Suniti Kumar Chatterji, 'Polyglottism in Indo-Aryan', forming Appendix II to 'Indo-Aryan and Hindi', Second edition, Calcutta, 1960, pp. 288–303, reprinted 1969.

226, *l.* 25: *add*: The anusvāra, which was originally a nasal continuation of the preceding vowel sound pronounced pure and without any nasal accompaniment, became quite early in the MIA stage transformed into a pure nasal,—a ङ् (ṅ), a न् (n), a म् (m) or a nasalized वँ् (w̃), and one or the other of these pronunciations has now been generalized in the different NIA languages. Thus it is now a full ঙ «ṅ» in Bengali, a «w̃» or «ũ» in Oriya, a न «n» in Bihar and North India, a वँ «w̃» also in Gujarat and Maharashtra, and a pure म «m» in the Dravidian-speaking South, in pronouncing Sanskrit words. In Old Bengal inscriptions, the use of ঙ «ṅ» generally for the anusvāra is indicative of this guttural nasal transformation becoming established in proto-Bengali; but we have the use of न «n» also, in an inscription like the Guṇāighar Inscription of Vainya-gupta, e.g. «trayō-vinśati, trinśa» for «-viṁsati, triṁśa» (c. A.D. 507).

232, *l.* 7: *read* rasūla *and* mōhāmōti; *l.* 20, *read* pūsĕ *for* pusĕ.

233: *immediately before* § **126**, *add*: Bengali MSS. in the Persian character are but rarely found in other parts of the country. One such MS., however, came to light some years ago—a Bengali version of the 'Qissah-i-Amīr Hamzah'—from Jessore district. It was exhibited by Maulavi

'Abdul-Wali in the ASB (November 1925). In its transcription, unlike the Chittagong MSS., it employs regularly ꠌ and ꠎ for চ and জ.

235, *heading, read*: SILĒṬ; *footnote, l.* 4, *read* in *for* is.

235, *Footnote, last four lines*:

These lines were written in 1926. I have since completely changed my opinion (by 1956) on the adoption of the Nagari script for all our Indian languages. Experience has shown, after India's Independence was achieved in 1947, while working as a Member of the 21-man 'Official Language Commission' set up by the Free Government of India in 1955 (with a view to find out ways and means to establish Hindi as the 'National' or 'Official' Language of India in place of English), and as Chairman of the 7-man Government of India Sanskrit Commission in 1956, that the question of this 'National Language' (Rāṣṭra-bhāṣā) and a national script for the whole of India may soon become a political issue, with a parochial undercurrent for the special benefit of certain groups, which was all the more anti-national and dangerous as it combined self-interest with patriotism; and moreover it was based on sentiment and not on a scientific and a national approach taking sympathetic note of all the various problems and difficulties affecting the entire country as a Union of Diverse Languages and Cultures and not as a Monolingual Nation. I now strongly support immediate *biliteralism*, with the various 'provincial' scripts and the Roman side by side, ultimately aiming at a slow and gradual change over to the Roman. The use of the Nagari is fraught with very great difficulties, for a language like Bengali or Tamil, and it is apprehended it will seek to perpetuate the undesirable domination of Hindi over all Indian languages which is emphatically against National Integration in India, taking note of the realities of the situation.

PHONOLOGY

240, *footnote, l.* 8, *add after* Transitional MIA Periods: Mention is to be made of a new discovery of a fragmentary Asoka inscription from Kandahar in 1963 in two languages—in Asoka's court language—the Magadhan Prakrit, transcribed in Aramaic or Syrian characters as current in Eastern Iran in the third century B.C., given in bits (with a few words at a time), followed by an Aramaic translation after each bit in the Indian language. These fragments of Asokan Prakrit in Aramaic script throws some light on the pronunciation of the former. See in this connexion the 'Journal Asiatique', Vol. 254, Year 1966, Fascicules 3–4: 'Une Inscription indo-araméenne d'Asoka provenant de Kandahar (Afghanistan)', by Emile Benveniste and André Dupont-Sommer, pp. 437–65, and 'La Séquence *SHYTY*' by Colette Caillat, pp. 467–70.

244, *l*. 25: OIA [ɦaãsa, ɦʌʌ̃sʌ], in Bengali [ɦɔŋʃo], Hindi [ɦʌns], Marathi [ɦʌʌ̃s], in the Dravidian languages [ɦʌmsʌ]. (See Suniti Kumar Chatterji: 'The Pronunciation of Sanskrit', K. B. Pathak Commemoration Volume, Bhandarkar Oriental Research Institute, Poona, 1934, pp. 330–49; and also in the Turner Volume of the 'Indian Linguistics', Vol. XXI; and 'Phonetic Transcriptions, etc., in the Study of Indian Languages', 'Indian Linguistics', XXII, Taraporewala Volume, Bombay, 1957.

245, *l*. 22, *read* tzándanon *for* tsándanon.

247, *l*. 18: « pã̆cila » < « *pañcila, < *paccīla = prācīra ».

251, *l*. 19: Thus in the 'Ṛk-prātiśākhya', VI, 5, we have the term « abhinidhāna » = « saṃdhāraṇa » *holding on*, for this phenomenon: see also W. D. Whitney, 'Atharva-Vēda-Prātiśākhya', pp. 38, 39. The terms « sanna-tara » *very weak, feeble, very depressed, etc.*, and « pīḍita » *pressed, suppressed, obscured, badly pronounced* were used in the 'Prātiśākhyas' for this kind of 'unexploded stop pronunciation' in late OIA.

254, 255: *loss of* « -tr- > -tt- »: W. Geiger cites also ('Festschrift E. Kuhn', p. 186), Sinhalese « hū » (sūtra), « mū » (mūtra), « rā » (rātri).

255: *after l.* 16 *of* § 135, *add*:

In the above cases of supposed simplification of double consonants to a single one (or of shortening of a 'long' consonant) in Early MIA, it seems quite certain that the matter was not phonetic but graphic. Thus in Asokan Brahmi, OIA « varṣa », which could have been pronounced in the third century B.C. (in other areas excepting the North-West) only as « vassa (or vaśśa) », was written as « vă̄sa » or « vāsa », both indicating the pronunciation « vassa ». This hesitancy in early Brahmi orthography was the result of an imperfect system of writing. Thus we have « kă̄sati » beside « kāsati », both standing for a pronunciation

« *kassati = OIA *karṣyati < kariṣyati ». The current orthography of Brahmi did not have double consonants, and the double consonant (or 'long' consonant) pronunciation was ambiguously indicated either by a short vowel + a single consonant, or by a long vowel + a single consonant. Further instances would be— « dharma > dhamma », written « dhaṁ-ma », also « dhā-ma » and « dhă-ma »; « rajjuka-, lajjuka- », written « rā-jū-kā » beside « lă-ju-ke = lajjuke »; « cikitsā > cikicchā », written « ci-kī-chā »; « rātri > ratti », written « ră-ti »; « dīrgha > diggha », written « dī-gha, dĭ-gha = NIA dīgha-lạ, dīghī, », etc.; « brāhmaṇa » > « bamhaṇa, babbhaṇa », written « bā-bha-ṇa, bă-bha-ṇa », NIA (Bihar) « bābhan »; « āgatya > āgacca » *having come*, written « ā-gā-ca ». Elsewhere, in other early Brahmi writing, spellings like these occur: « vā-ṭa » for « vaṭṭa = vartman », « gā-bha, gă-bha = gabbha < garbha », « sī-dha = siddha », « mī-ta = mitta < mitra », « ă-gi, ā-gi = aggī < agni- », « jā-bu for jambu », « dā-ta for datta », « sā-ta-mī » for « sattamī < saptamī », « va-chi » for « vacchī < vātsī », « bha-yā » for « bhayyā < bhāryā », « ā-na » for « anna < anya », « na-da » for « nanda », « Ga-ga » for « Gagga < Garga, Gārgya », « rā-ta» for « ratta < rakta », etc. Such spellings are found all over Aryan India,—Western, Northern, Eastern,—during the early centuries of Brahmi writing. As in a few of the examples quoted above, the group, short vowel+nasal+stop, is also at times written as a vowel (short or long)+stop, omitting the nasal.

Although one consonant was the rule in writing, in pronunciation the consonant was invariably doubled, as it is clear from the later development of NIA from MIA. But it is likely that in later Prakrit, after a more systematized orthography became established for both Sanskrit and the Prakrits (e.g. in Gupta Brahmi of *c.* A.D. 400, and in the Siddhamātṛkā of the time of Harṣa-vardhana, *c.* A.D. 630), some old-fashioned unphonetic spellings seem to have found a place in Sanskrit and Prakrit orthography, like « dīgha, rāti, mūta, sūta » for « diggha, ratti, mutta, sutta », etc., which have become in NIA regularly « dīgha-, rāt-, mūt-, sūt- », etc. But in a few cases, the wrong spellings brought in a new 'spelling pronunciation', with the result that « dīgha » gave a false form « dīha » in later Prakrit, and possibly Sinhalese « rā, mū, hū » originated from these 'spelling pronunciations'. See also 'A Note on the Orthography of the Early Brāhmī Inscriptions in the matter of Indication of the Double Consonants' by Suniti Kumar Chatterji, appended at the end of Professor U. N. Ghoshal's article 'Asokan Studies', in his 'The Beginnings of Indian Histriography, and other Essays', Calcutta, 1944, pp. 82–84, first published in the IHQ, Dec., 1930.

256, *l.* 21: « ratta (< ratna) » actually occurs in MIA (in the Pali 'Sutta-nipāta, Sabhiya-sutta': « ratta-ñña » = « ratna-jña », explained in the Commentary of Buddha-ghosa as « ratana-ññu »).

259, *bottom of page*: Interesting side-light regarding the pronunciation of Old Bengali (and medieval Sanskrit in Eastern India) will be found in Hackin's 'Formulaire Sanscrit-tibetain', giving a Sanskrit text as pronounced and written in the Tibetan Script. Giuseppe Tucci in his review of the present work (ODBL) in the 'Modern Review', Calcutta, for January 1927, pp. 45–46, has observed in a footnote as follows: 'For the pronunciation of ancient Bengali many an important hint can be had from a Sanskrit text transliterated into Tibetan which has been published by Hackin, *Formulaire Sanscrit-tibetain.*'

260, *l.* 25: *read* « -vā » for « -ā ».

263, *l.* 18: *read* ʃ̊i(ĕ)a:la *for* ʃi(ĕ)a:la.

264, *l.* 14: *read* kofii *for* kŋhi; *l.* 17: *read* cʃupoṛi *for* cʃupaṛi.

265, *l.* 5, *from bottom*: *read* mɒnɒ, *with* न = « n » *instead of* ण = « ṇ ».

269, *l.* 3, *from bottom, add*: The glottal stop occurs with the voiced stops and palatal or dental affricates [g', ɟʒ' (ʤ'), ḍ', d', b'] in most East Bengali dialects as the regular substitutes for the corresponding aspirates [gɦ, ɟʒɦ, ḍɦ, dɦ, bɦ] of Standard Bengali.

270, *after line* 8, *add*: The treatment of « h = ɦ » and the voiced aspirated stops in many of the East Bengali dialects is a noteworthy feature of the Modern Bengali Phonetics and Phonology. This was omitted in 1926 in the ODBL, as the matter was not studied or known at that time. See *ante*, Notes on *ll.* 4, 5, *page* 143.

272, *l.* 18: *Correct* 2.02 *to* 0.02.

277, *l.* 26: *add at the end within the brackets*: Cf. also Banarsidas Jain, 'Stress Accent in Indo-Aryan', BSOS, London, IV, 2, pp. 315–23.

278, *ll.* 7, 8: The OIA source of the word « derkho » (which has been also wrongly printed in some published books as ডেল্‌কো « ḍēlkō ») is « dīpa-vṛkṣa- »; it is also called in Bengali দীপ-গাছা « dīpa-gāchā » also meaning *lamp-tree.*

286, *add at the end of the page*:

I have since found out that the Payār, or Lāchāḍi (or Lesārī, in Assamese) as a verse-metre ignoring length of vowels as a measure and having only 8 short syllables in the first part of the line and 6 short syllables or 4 short+1 long syllable in the second part, occurs also in Bhojpuri and in Maithili (information and specimens through the kindness of Professor Uday Narayan Tiwari for Bhojpuri in 1942, and of Pandit Devananda Jha Vedaratna for Maithili in 1943).

In Bhojpuri, this metre is called 'Maharā', or 'Maharāī'. It is quite different in cadence from the usual forms of 'mātrā-vṛtta' or moric metres of both Bhojpuri and Maithili.

Bhojpuri: « sumiru su/miru mana //sirajana-hāra//
jinha kaila/ sura nara //saraga patāra// »

Think, O my mind, think of the Creator—
He who made gods and men, and heaven and the abysmal regions.

« eka dina/ mana mŏrā//caṛhala pahāra//
gāī-ke ga/harī dekhi//bahuta pasāra//
aganita/gāī bhāī// gani na sirāī//
duhu disa/gō-dhana//rahe chiti chāī// »

One day my mind ascended a hill :
I saw a gathering of cattle, widely extended.
Countless cows, brothers, one cannot count them :
Cows, our wealth, on both sides, were there covering the earth.

—(from a Bhojpuri poem by Dharaṇī-dāsa)

Maithili: « kalita ku/śala baka/// Kōilakha gēla//
kaṭahara/ caṛhi ĕka//kurasā lēla// »

A wily and clever heron went to Koilakh (a village),
Mounting on a jack-fruit tree, he took a Kurasā fish.

287, *ll.* 11, 12: It should be noted that the «Payār» has also 16 *morae*, including the pauses, although the number of syllables is 14.

288, *footnote, add*: Cf. Ramesh Chandra Basu, 'Payār-chandēr Utpatti', in the VSPdP for Bengali year 1311 (= 1904), pp. 148–60.

289: Versification in Bengali, Stressed Metre.

A number of Bengali scholars have been working on the nature and history of Bengali metrics for some decades, and although there has not been a complete agreement both as regards history and technical analysis of Bengali verse styles, as well as the technical terms, and as regards matters of detail, the basic points have now become clear. The following bibliography of important papers and books in Bengali on the subject since 1926 will give the various points of view:

1. Rabindranath Tagore: 'Chanda': First edition, July 1936; Enlarged edition, Visva-Bharati, November 1962, p. 571.
2. Tarapada Bhattacharyya: 'Chandō-vijñāna': Calcutta, B.G. Printers and Publishers Ltd., September 1948, p. 282.
3. Mohitlal Majumdar: 'Bāṅglā Kabitār Chanda,' Vanga-bharati Library, Calcutta, 2nd edition, 1955.
4. Amulyadhan Mukhopadhyay: 'Bāṅglā Chandēr Mūla-Sūtra', Calcutta University, 5th edition, 1957.
5. Sudhibhushan Bhattacharyya: 'Bāṅglā Chanda,' Calcutta, M. C. Sarkar & Sons (Private) Ltd., 1962, p. 274.
6. Prabodh Chandra Sen: 'Chanda-parikramā', Calcutta, 'Jijñāsā', May 1965, p. 140.
7. Dilip Kumar Ray: 'Chāndasikī': Calcutta University, 1968, pp. 290+16.
8. Ananda Mohan Basu: 'Bāṅglā Padābalīr Chanda', Bolpur, Dist. Birbhum, July 1968, p. 518.

—(Fuller bibliographies in Nos. 6 and 8)

292, *l.* 23: *after* the stress *add*: and to a fixed number of syllables.

292, *l.* 31: The lines quoted below (and in the next page) are not in pure stressed metre (svara-vṛtta chandaḥ), as erroneously suggested in the text—but they are in the native Bengali type of moric metre (mātrā-vṛtta).

293, *l.* 6: *read* bãcʃia *for* bâcʃia.

294, *l.* 12: *read* cʃa(ĕ)e *for* ca(ĕ)e.

298, *l.* 6: *read* 'ʃa͡ɟʒɔ *for* ʃa͡ɟʒə.

301, § **149**, *l.* 4: *before* এক « ēkȧ », *add* ইঁদ « ĩdȧ » *Indra* (in Bankura District).

301, *last line*: *read* pātȧ *for* pātå.

302, *l.* 20: *read* kåṛā *for* kărā.

302, *l.* 27: *after* (kālaka): *add* so গোরো রঙ « gōrō (< gōra + uā) raṅ » *fair colour*, cf. গোরো মেয়ে « gōrō mēyē » *fair girl*, in Birbhum district, beside গোরা « gōrā » *the fair or white one, a European, an English soldier*; and গোরা « Gōrā » *a name of Chaitanya-deva (because of his fair complexion).*

304, *l.* 22: *add also* পানীয় « pānīya » *potable.*

305, *after l.* 13 *add*:

A final « -a » in *ts.* words transforms these words into *stss.* by being changed in Colloquial Bengali to « -i » or « -u » in disyllabic words when the first syllable has « i » or « u » : e.g. « iṣṭa > iṣṭi, piṇḍa > piṇḍi, siṃha > siṅghi, miṣṭa > miṣṭi, mitra > *mittri > mittir, citra > *cittri > cittir »; also « caritra > *carittri > carittir », a trisyllabic word; so « duṣṭa > duṣṭu, muṇḍa > muṇḍu, kuṇḍa > kuṇḍu, tuṣṭa > tuṣṭu, mūrkha > mukkhu, sūkṣma > sukkhũ, dhūrta > dhuttu, ūrdhva > *tbh.* ubbha > ubhu », etc.

Final « -a » preceded by a « y », or by « kṣ » and « jñ » (in Bengali pronunciation « khya, gyã »), in *tss*, becomes « -i » : « yajña > yaggĩ, jaggi; pathya > pathyi, patthi; satya > sattyi, satti; lakṣa > lakkhya, lakkhi; sūryya = sūrjya > surjji, sujji » (spelt as সুয্যি « sūyyi »), etc.

306, *l.* 12: Other examples of « -ā > -ă > zero »: OIA গোধা « gōdhā > MIA gōhā > Bengali gōh, gō » (as in গোসাপ « gō-sāpȧ » *iguana*); ঘটা « ghaṭā > ghaḍā > MB ঘড় ghaṛȧ » *array*, as in Krittivāsa; যাত্রা « yātrā > jattā, jattă > যাত, জাত jātȧ » as in জাত-গান « jātȧ-gānȧ (Manbhum District) = yātrā-gāna » *song and play* and in মহানাদের জাত « Mahānāderȧ jātȧ » for « Mahānādēra yātrā » *a festival in a village near Magra in West Bengal (Hugli Dt.).*

309, *l.* 8: *read* MB *for* MA.

312, *l.* 7: Cf. also পই-পই (ক'রে) বলা « paï-paï (ka'rē) balā » *to repeat at every step, to repeat or warn continually*: « padē padē = pratipadam ».

313, *l.* 11: *after* (alābu), *add:* হেঁট « hẽṭa » *below* > *in a crouching position* (*ahẽṇṭa < *aheṭṭha < *adhiṣṭāt, Buddhist Sanskrit heṣṭā = OIA adhastāt) ; MB পাসরে « pāsare » *forgets* (apa-smarati).

314, *after l.* 29: Other examples of initial « a-+one consonant » changing to « ā »: « amṛṣṭa- » *not swept or cleaned* (as opposed to sam-mṛṣṭa = *cleaned*) > * « aw̃iṭṭha- > ā̃iṭhā—ā̃iṭhuā > ẽṭhō, ẽṭō » *uncleaned, as of plates after a meal, or touched with lips*; « ali-jihvā > আলজিভ āl-jibha, āl-jib(h)a » *uvula*; « agni > MIA *sts.* agani > আগনি, আগুনি, আগুন āgani, āguni, āguna » *fire* ; আবোলা « ā-bolā » *not speaking, without speech* > অবলা « a-balā », e.g. গোরু অবলা জীব « gōru abalā jība » *a cow is an animal without language* (this « abalā » is mistakenly taken to mean *weak, powerless*: but cf. Modern Greek, in which a horse—« *hippos* » in Standard or Old Greek—is usually called « alogos (aloγo) » = *without speech*); « aputra > avutta, avuṭṭa > *avuṇṭa, āvuṇṭa > Bengali আউঁট « āũṭa » as in আউঁট-কুড়া, আঁটকুড়ো « āũṭa-kuṛā, ā̃ṭa-kuṛō » *one with a home* (kuṛā = kūṭa) *without a son* ; cf. Panjabi « aũt, aut » *without issue.*

315, *l.* 19: *read* maśāna *for* masāna.

316, *l.* 12: *read* « ā̃ta » *for* « āta »; *after* (antra), *add:* আশথ beside অশথ « āśatha, aśatha (aśvattha) »; *and in l.* 15, *delete*: খাজা « khājā » *a sweet-meat to be chewn* (khādya), *and take this deleted portion to* p. 321, *l.* 23, *before the word* জাড় ; *adding* khăjja *before* khādya.

319, *l.* 20: The word « sabhā » forming the plural. Dr. Sukumar Sen has drawn my attention to the word « yuvati-sabhā » in Song 18 of the 'Gīta-Gōvinda' (Canto IX). Cf. also pp. 732–33.

319, *l.* 21: The form সব « saba < MIA sarvva, sabba < OIA sarva ». A connexion with « sabhā » *assemblage, gathering*, as suggested by Dr. Sukumar Sen, has been noted. Helmer Smith, in the 'Bulletin de la Société de Linguistique de Paris', 1935, Vol. 36, fasc. 1, p. 18, has discussed the question of the aspirated form. Rev. S. H. Kellogg, 'A Grammar of the Hindi Language', § 330, has referred to « sabhõ » as oblique plural, as opposed to « sab », nominative, case direct, singular. Jules Bloch, 'Langue Marathe', Paris, p. 133, also considered the « bh » in « sabh » as being from « sarva > savva > sab-+-h ». Helmer Smith regards « sabhõ » as being an aggregative form, like « dōnõ, tinõ », which are morphologically connected with oblique plurals like « unhō̃, kinhō̃, jinhō̃ (= Braj jinhaũ) », etc. MIA (Apabhraṁśa) « savvahā̃ » should have given « *sā̃bā̃ » (cf. Braj « jā-kaũ, jā-hi < jaha- »). « sabh » may be explained as a back formation: e.g. « lōg-ō̃ > lōg (nom.) », so « sabhō̃ > sabh ». « jinhō̃ », etc., are to be analysed not as « jin-h-ō̃ », but as « jin-hō̃ », the « -hō̃ » being taken ready-made from « (-a)-hō̃ < -aha(n)am ». Dialectal Bengali forms like সভান, সভানের « sabhāna̍, sabhānēra̍ » *of all*, are, however, extensions of সভ « sabha », whatever is its origin. We may also note the Gujarati form « sāv < savva » *complete*.

With regard to the phonological problem « vartatē > vaṭṭaï > Bengali বটে baṭe, Oriya aṭē », compare Bhojpuri « bāṛē < *bāṭē » (« bāṭē » would be regular from « vaṭṭatī, vartatē »), plural « bāṛan (vartantē) », and also « bāe, bāy, bā », which show the final phonetic decay of this verb.

320, *l.* 3: cf. নিশিভোর « niśi-bhōra̍ » *for the whole night* < « niśi+bhara »: cf. দিন-ভর, রাত-ভর, মাস-ভর, বছর-ভর « dina̍-bhara̍, rāta̍-bhara̍, māsa̍-bhara̍, bachara̍-bhara̍ », etc. Cf. also MIA « nisi-bharammi » (PSM). Here « bhōra » with « -ō- » may be through the influence of the word ভোর « bhōra̍ » *dawn, early morning = the whole night up to dawn.*

321, *l.* 8: পগার « pagāra »: probably Persian « paigār » *ditch.* Is it Hindustani Persianized, or *vice versa*?

321, *ll.* 16, 17: The earlier form of নায়ের, also found in dialectal Bengali, is নাইঅর, নাইহর « nāi(h)ara̍ ».

322, *l.* 13: *add*: The reverse process of « ē; i > ē > æ > ā » with nasals or nasalization of the vowel, is also found: Sanskrit « ḍayana- » *flying*, Hindi « ḍainā » Bengali ডেনা, ড্যানা, ডানা « ḍēnā, ḍyānā = ḍænā (dialectal), (Standard) ḍānā » *wing*; « chidra- > chidda-, *chinda- » Bengali ছেঁদা, ছ্যাঁদা, ছাঁদা « chē̃dā, chæ̃dā > chā̃dā » *hole*; « gendā » *marigold*, as in Hindi = Bengali গেঁদা, গ্যাঁদা, গাঁদা « gē̃dā, gæ̃dā, gā̃dā »; « sandhi » *piercing* (*through the wall*) > « *sendhi » > Bengali সিঁধ « sī̃dha̍ », also verb সেঁধানো, সাঁধানো « sē̃dhānō, sā̃dhānō » *enter, wriggle in.*

324, *l.* 3: দেরখো « dēra̍khō »: *see ante, Note on p.* 278, *ll.* 7, 8. *Also p.* 331, *l.* 16.

324, *l.* 6: *read* « niṣuti » *for* « niṣuṭi »; *l.* 10, *read* * piuśī *for* pīuśī; *l.* 25, *read* টীঁঠ *for* টীঠ.

325, *l.* 10, *read* *ūru *for* *uru; *l.* 21, *read* -aṣṭhi- *for* -asthi-.

328, *l.* 8, *after* (rēkhā) *add*: whence Modern Bengali (as in Murshidabad District) র‍্যা [ræ:] *furrow-line, plough-track.*

328, *l.* 28: *add* বেসাতি, বেসাত « bēsāti, bēsāta » *business, buying and selling* (vaiśya-tva-); সেঁঝুতি « sẽjhuti » *evening lamp* (sandhyā-vartikā).

329, *l.* 8 *from bottom*: *correct* bōḍra *to* bōḍra.

331, *l.* 20, *read* যদ্দিন *for* যদিন; *l.* 25, *read* caritavya *for* cartavya.

331, *l.* 21: *add* বড়-ঠাকুর > বট্‌ঠাকুর « baḍa-ṭhākura > baṭa-ṭhākura » *title of respect for husband's elder brother.* *l.* 31: cf. also গুরুঠাকুর « guru-ṭhākura » *respected (spiritual) teacher* > গুর্‌ ঠাকুর, গুট্‌ ঠাকুর (extreme colloquial form) « gura-ṭhākura > guṭa-ṭhākura ».

333, *l.* 8: *after* [ʃidne], *add*: ঘটীটা « ghaṭī-ṭā » *that water vessel,* বাটীটা « bāṭī-ṭā » *that cup* = Standard Coll. ঘট্‌টে, বাট্‌টে « ghōṭaṭē, bāṭaṭē ».

334, *ll.* 5, 6: Alternative derivation— « prativēśya > (Pali) paṭivĕssa-, paṭivissa-, (Old Bengali) পঁডিশি paḍiśi > Bengali পড়শি paṛaśi; = Hindi paṛōs ».

334, *l.* 7: *from bottom, add*: করম্‌চা < *করমছা < *করমোছা « karamacā < *kara-machā < *kara-mōchā » *an acid fruit, Cassia carondas* (Skt. kara-marda, Hind. karaundā: cf. 'Devatā', Panini Office, Allahabad, 1917, p. 155).

334, *l.* 14: also, *sts.* ভাগিনা, ভাগনে « bhāginā, bhāganē < *bhāginaa < bhāgi-nēya ».

334, *l.* 21: *add*: strong initial stress in a sense-unit or breath-unit as part of a sentence has given rise to wide-spread loss of interior « -ē- », leading to a sort of polysynthesis or holophrasis in Modern Colloquial Bengali: e.g. যাইতে দেও > যেতে দাও > যেদ্দাও, জেদ্দাও « jāitē dēō > jētē-dāo > jēddāo » *let it go*; বসিয়া থাকিয়া > ব'সে থেকে > ব'স্‌ থেকে « basiyā thākiyā > ba'sē thēkē > ba's-thēkē » *while sitting, or while remaining seated*; শুখাইতে দিতে > শুখোতে, শুখুতে দিতে > শুকুদ্দিতে « śukhāïtē-ditē > 'śukhōtē, śukhutē ditē > śukudditē » *to let it dry*; এ-বেলা, ও-বেলা > এব্‌লা, ওব্‌লা « ē-bēlā, ō-bēlā > ēblā, ōblā » *this time of the day, that time of the day*, etc.

335, *l.* 7: *from bottom*: *correct* persons *to* person.

335, *l.* 21: cf. Pali « mutinga < mṛdaṅga; kaḷimbhaka < kaḍamba *point*; pilāla < palāla ».

336, *l.* 9: *add* ময়ান « mayāna » *extra ghee* (*or oil*) *mixed with flour* (*to make pastry soft and melt in the mouth*), originally *oil, wax or butter rubbed* *on lips during winter*: 'Karpūra-mañjarī', I, verse 13: « bimboṭṭhē bahalaṁ ṇa denti maaṇaṁ ṇō gandha-tellāvilā » *they do not put any more* maaṇa *to their* bimba-*like lips, nor are they using perfumed oil* (« maaṇa = OIA *mradana, mṛdana, mradā » *soft* < « mṛdu »: in Hindi « moyān », Garhwali « mōṇ », Nepali « mayan, maĩn », Marathi « mo(h)aṇ »).

337, *l.* 10: *correct* -ũ- *to* -ŭ-.

337, *l.* 12: The source of চৌধুরী « caudhurī » may equally be « catur-dhara-ikå »: cf. Hindi, Maithili etc., « caudh(a)rī », Assamese « caudhāri ».

341, *l.* 6: *from bottom*: *read* ʃɑĕr *for* ʃaĕr.

342, *l.* 10: *read* chāẏårā *for* chāẏåṛā; *l.* 19, *delete* MB.

342, *l.* 16: *after* (vadana), *add*: ময়ান « mayānå » (mradana): *see above, note on page* 336, *l.* 9.

345, *ll.* 5, 6: In the 'Varṇa-ratnākara', we have Early Maithili « mahuari ». which would suggest « *madhu+karikā » as the source of মৌহারী « mauhārī ».

347, *l.* 31: *also* প'ল, প'লো, পোলো « pa'la, pa'lō, pōlō » *bamboo basket to catch fish*, Assamese « pala » < « palava < plava »; বলদ « baladå » *ox, draught ox* (balī-varda > *balivadda, *balavadda): cf. Ass. « kācha = kāso (kacchapa, kacchava); Bhāda (Bhādrapada, Bhaddavaa); pāra (pārāvata, *pāravaa); gādha (gardabha, gaddaha) ». NB দম্বল « dambalå » *sour milk or lemon juice, to turn milk into curds*, < « OIA dadhi+amla > dadhy-ambla > *dahi-amb(a)la, *daï-ambala, *dayambalå > *daambala, dambalå »; cf. also Skt. *ts.* « apacaya » *waste*, in Cal. Coll. অপ্চ « apåca < *apacaa »; Skt. « ā-śakti » *might, power, ability*, « ā-śakta- » *very powerful, mighty, able* (= samyak-śakti-viśiṣṭa, as in a late lexicon) > « āsatta-a > āsåtå > NB আস্ত āsta, MB also অস্তা āstā » *unbroken, uncut, whole, entire* (? : cf. English *whole* < *hale*).

348, *l.* 27. *Also* কাল-সাপ « kālå-sāpå » *black snake, cobra*, কাল-নাগিনী « kālå-nāginī » *black female snake*, কালকূট « kālå-kūṭå » *a virulent poison*; কাল-পেঁচা « kālå-pẽcā » *black owl*, কাল-কচু « kālå-kacu » *black or bitter yam*; কাল-কাশুন্দা « kālå-kāśundā » *black* kāśundā *plant*, etc. Comparable to কাল্, কাল (কালো), কালা « kālå, kālō, kālā », we have other words like ভাল্, ভাল (ভালো), ভালা « bhālå (as in ভাল-মানুষী > ভাল্-মান্‌ষি « bhāla-mānuṣī > bhāl-mānṣi » *behaving like a good or honest man*, ভালো মানুষ « bhālō mānuṣȧ » *a good man*, ভালা মোর বাপা « bhālā mōrȧ bāpā » *good father mine* (*in familiar jocular spirit, addressing a friend in appreciation*); কাঁচা « kā̃cā » *not ripe*, but কাঁচ-কলা « kā̃cȧ-kalā » *unripe banana*; ঘোড় « ghōṛȧ » *horse* as in ঘোড়-দৌড় « ghōṛȧ-dauṛȧ » *horse-race*, beside ঘোড়া « ghōṛā » *horse*. Cf. the *short*, *ordinary*, *long*, *and redundant* forms of Western and Central Magadhan speeches—« ghur (ghŏr); ghōrā; ghŏrawā; ghŏrauwā ».

349, *l.* 1: *after* NIA, *add*: (where no special force of the « -ā- » is present or evident).

350, *l.* 4: *before* etc. *add*: যাই, তাই « jāi, tāi » (yadā-hi, tadā-hi).

350, *after line* 12, *add*: In a few instances, we have « -āva » > ও « -ō » in Bengali: ধোয় « dhōy, dhōĕ » *washes* (dhāvati: possibly influence of « dhauta > *dhōta) »; তো, ত', ত « tō, ta', ta = tō » (tāvat) *indeed, truly, verily* (different from the other তো « tō » from « tataḥ, tatō, tadō, *taō, *taü » meaning *then ?*, *what then ?*)

350, *l.* 20: *delete* দেউল « dēulȧ » (MIA dēula, dēva-kula).

350, *l.* 24: *add* একুন « ekunȧ » *total, totality, in all* (ēka+pūrṇa > -uṇṇa: cf. Hindi ikaunā); বাছুর « bāchurȧ » *calf* (vatsa-rūpa, vaccha-rūa, bācharū > bāchaur, bāchur); so গাভুর « gābhurȧ » *youth, young man* (garbha-rūpa).

351, *l.* 13: *add at the end*: But পৌনে « paune, poune » *less by a quarter* has « -au- » for MIA « -āo- » (pāoṇa < pādōna).

352, *l.* 15: *read* *duulia *for* *duūlia; *l.* 8 *from bottom, after* (dēva, dēha), *add*: রে, র‍্যা [re:, ræ:] *track-line for plough to follow* (*rēa, rēha, rēhā, rēkhā).

352, *l.* 15: *delete* দুলী, *etc.*

352: *after l.* 24, *add*: In Calcutta Bengali, « -uā » is further contracted to « -ō »: e.g. জুআ, জুও, জো « jŭā > jō » (dyūta-); কুআ, কুয়া, কুও, কো « kuyā=kuwā, kuō, kō » (kūpa-); *কান-কুআ, কানকুও, কান্‌কো « kāna-kuā, kāna-kuō, kānakō » *gills of fish* (karṇa-kūpa-); দুহা, দুআ, দুও, দো « du(h)-ā, dō » (durbhagā- > duhā); সুহা, সুআ, সুও, সো « su(h)ā-, suō, sō » (subhagā- > suhā-); *বাঘা-ভালুকুআ ; বাঘা-ভাল্‌কো « bāghā-bhāluk-uā > bāghā-bhālakō » *like a big tiger or bear* (vyāghra-+bhalluka+uā).

352, *after l.* 29, *add*: Old Bengali « bīyaṇa- » (= Skt. vīraṇa-) > « *beaṇa-, Modern Bengali বেনা bēnā » *an aromatic shrub*, '*khus-khus*'. Middle Bengali « ēā » from various sources becomes in the Calcutta colloquial [æĕ], e.g. বেহালা, ব্যায়লা « behālā, beyālā [bæĕlaa] » *violin* (from Portuguese viola ?); পেয়ারা > প্যায়রা « peārā [pæĕraa] » *a pear, a guava* (from Portuguese pera); পেয়ালা, প্যালা « pēyālā, pyālā [pæĕlaa] » *cup* (from Persian pyālah); জেয়াদা, জ্যাদা, জ্যায়দা « jēādā, jyādā [ɟʒæedaa] » (Perso-Arabic zyādah) *too much*; দেহালা, দেয়ালা « dē(h)ālā [dæĕlaa] »; *a baby's smile in sleep* (? dēva-kalā-, dēva-khēlā-); শেহালা, শেয়ালা, শ্যায়লা « śē(h)ālā [ʃæĕlaa] » *moss, slime in a mass of water or in a moist place* (śaibāla-), found also as শ্যাওলা [ʃæŏlaa]; Skt. « pārāvata-, Pali pārēpata » *pigeon* = Bengali পায়রা [paaĕraa]: here the vocalism is not clear (? pārāvata > *pāraua > *pārwā > *pā?rā > pāyrā).

353, *l.* 7: *from bottom*: *read* *ghrata.

353, *after l.* 7: *add*: So « gōdhā > gōhā̆ > *gōa- > Bengali গো gō- » as in গোসাপ « gō-sāpȧ » *iguana* (= gōdhā-sarpa; Dialectal Bengali গুহিল « guhilȧ [g'uil] », *ibid.*, = Rajasthani « gōhil- »; Middle Bengali « ōā » from various sources becomes in the Calcutta colloquial [ɔ:, ɔĕ] = like English *au* as in *caught*, e.g. Standard Bengali গোয়ালা « gōālā (gōpāla-) = Calcutta Bengali গয়লা « gayȧlā [gɔĕlɑ] », Calcutta Bengali ময়রা mayȧrā [mɔĕrɑ-] *a pastry cook* (mōdaka-kara- > *mōaaara- > *mōāra-); ওহাড়, ওয়াড় « ō(h)āṛȧ » *pillow-case* = অড় [ɔ : ṛ], (avavēṣṭa- ?); দোয়াৎ « dōātȧ » *ink-pot* (Perso-Arabic dawāt) = দৎ [dɔ : t]; রওয়াক, রোয়াক « raōākȧ, rōāk » (Persian rawāq) *ledge of house* = রক্ [rɔ : k]; Perso-Arabic « waqt » *time*, « walī » *ruler, teacher*, « wazū » *ablutions*, « wasil » *a name*, « wazed » *a name* = ওক্ত or অক্ত, অলী, অজু, অছেল, অজেদ « ōkta or ȧkta, ȧlī, ȧjū, ȧchēl, ȧjēd »; দরওয়াজা « darōājā » *door* (Persian darwāzah) = দরজা « darȧjā », also দরোজা « darōjā »; Poetic Bengali মাতোয়ালা, মাতোয়ারা « mātōālā, -ārā » *intoxicated* (matta-pāla-), beside মাতল «(mātalȧ); and Sanskrit words like « svāda, svāmī » become সোয়াদ, সোয়ামী « sōādȧ, sōāmi » and then in extremely colloquial forms সদ্, সমী [ʃɔ:d, ʃɔmi]. So « anusvāra » became « *anussōāra », and then in common Bengali pronunciation [onuʃʃɔr], as if অনুস্বর; and শোভাবাজার « Śōbhā-bājārȧ », *name of one of the old quarters of North Calcutta*, first became [ʃoβabaɟʒɑr], with bilabial spirant [β] for aspirate [bɦ], and then [ʃoabaɟʒɑr], now actually pronounced as শ'-বাজার [ʃɔbaɟʒɑr]. So কাঁঠালের কোয়া « kā̃ṭhālērȧ kōā > -kȧ [kɔ:] » *the seed pod, seed vessel, sheath of the jack-fruit* (kōṣa-, kōha-, kōā); Sanskrit « samāṅga », Hindi « sa**w̃**āṅg, swāṅg », Bengali *সোআঙ্, সঙ্ « **sōāṅg > sȧṅ** » [ʃɔ:ŋ] ***disguise, fancy dress.***

355, *l.* 8: *after* (nacca, nṛtya), *add*: MB বাসোয়া « bāsōā » *ox, bull* = Maithili « basahā » (vasaha-, vṛṣabha-); *in l.* 21, *read* *tādṛśaṇa.

355, *l.* 28: *after* (ṛju), *add*: this is found in NB as a *sts.* as রুজু « ruju », e.g. « ruju-ruju jānālā, darajā » *windows or doors in a room opposite to each other.*

356, *l.* 2: *before* etc., *add* বুক « buka » *chest* (cf. Skt. vṛkka, Avestan vərəδka *kidney*, MIA bukka).

357, *l.* 5 *from bottom*: *correct* egreja *to* igreja.

357, *l.* 31: Other instances of consonant + « -ra, -ri » falling in line with ঋ « ṛ » in *stss.* and foreign words: e.g. বৃহৎ > বির্হৎ, বিরদ, বিরোদ « bṛhat > birhat, birada, birōda » *big*: প্রভু « prabhu > purbhu (as in the 'Crepar Xaxtrer Orthbhed') » *lord*; প্রয়াগ « Prayāga (= *Allahabad city*) > proĕāg > pŏĕrāg, pŏerāg, poirāg »; গ্রহণ « grahaṇa (> grehan, gerhòn > geron) » *eclipse of Sun or Moon*; পরমায়ু « paramāyu » *life-span* (pårmāĕu, promāi, pormāi, premāi, permāi); প্রলয় « pralaya » *dissolution of the universe, chaos, chaotic, vast* (prelaĕ, perlaĕ, pellăĕ, pellāĕ); প্রহ্লাদ « Prahlāda » *a Purana character* (prelhād > prellād + -iyā = prelhādiyā > pellādē = *a spoilt child*); Portuguese « Cristiaõ কৃস্তাউঁ > খ্রিস্তান, খ্রীষ্টান Khrīṣṭān » became খ্রেস্তান, খেষ্টান « Khrestān, Kheṣṭān », beside eighteenth century Bengali ক্রেস্তাওঁ « krestāõ » (English *Christian* gives current Bengali কৃশ্চান, ক্রিশ্চান Kriścān); Persian « Mīr-deh » *headman of a village* > Bengali surname written as মৃধা, মির্দা, মিদ্দা, মিদ্যা « mṛidhā, mirdā, midda, midyā ».

358, *l.* 3, *l.* 6: read respectively [aabritɔ] and [aabbritɔ]; *last line, correct to* ghanakam.

358, Nasalization of Vowels.

See in this connexion the monograph of Prof. Abdul Hai, 'A Phonetic and Phonological Study of Nasals and Nasalization in Bengali', University of Dacca, East Bengal, Pakistan, 1960, p. 241, which gives a descriptive or synchronistic study of nasals and nasalization in Bengali. As the treatment here is not historical and comparative, the question of Reduced Nasals in Bengali is not taken up (*see* pp. 360, 361, 362 in the ODBL).

359, *l.* 12: *for* « w̃ » *read* « ẇ ».

362, *l.* 27: There are exceptions, in affixes: e.g. in the present participle (śatṛ) forms in « -ant-, -nt- », the nasalization is lost in Bengali (*see*

p. 372 below), and in the locative affix for the noun, -ত, -তে « -ta, -tē < **-anta-**, -antahi » in MIA.

363, *l.* 12: *after* Bengal, *add*: In *tss.* and *stss.* in Calcutta Bengali, a pronunciation [ŋŋ] for [ŋg] is also common: e.g. গঙ্গাস্নান = [gɔŋŋɑsnɑn], সঙ্গে-সঙ্গে = [ʃɔŋŋeʃɔŋŋe], অঙ্গাঙ্গীভাবে = [ɔŋŋɑŋŋibɦɑbe] *in close proximity, limb-to-limb.*

364, *l.* 7, *add*: But we have the *sts.* বেন্নন « bennana (bennòn) » *curry* from « vyañjana ».

364, *l.* 14: *before* শিঙ্নি, *add* লাং (ল্যাং) মারা « lāṅ (læṅ) mārā » *to trip one with the foot or with a kick*, from « √laṅgh » *jump.*

365, *l.* 12: *read* ṣaṇḍa *for* saṇḍa.

365, *l.* 29: *add, as first example*: ইঁদ « Ĩda [ĩ:d] » *Indra*, common in Birbhum and West Bengal districts; e.g. ইঁদ রাজার অপ্সরী « Ĩda-rājāra apsarī » *an Apsaras of King Indra*; ইন্দাস, ইঁদাস « Indāsa, Ĩdāsa » (Indrāvāsa), *a village name*; ইঁদারা, ইঁদেরা « Ĩdārā, Ĩdērā » *a big masonry well with plenty of water* (Indrāgāra-); ইঁদকুড়ি, ইঁদুকুড়ি « Ĩda-kuṛi, Idu-kuṛi » *name of a quarter in Vishnupur town (in Bankura)* (Indra-kūṭikā, Indra-kuṇḍikā ?).

365, *l.* 32: *after* (bindu), *add*: *drop; drunken stupor*; পঁড়িত « pãṛita, *sts.* from paṇḍita », *title of a class of priests of the Dharma cult among the Ḍom caste.*

366, *l.* 7 *from bottom*: *read* śimula *for* śimulā.

367, *l.* 12 *add*: and SKK চাম্ভলী « cāmbhalī » *a flower* for « cāmēli ».

369, *l.* 7 *from bottom*: *read* *iṇṭa *for* *inṭa.

369, *l.* 23, *add at the end*: So early Bengali আচাভুআ « ācābhuā » *passing strange, wonderful* (atyadbhuta-, accabbhua-), beside Early Awadhi (as in Tulasidasa's 'Rama-carita-manasa') « acambhau » (with nasalization).

370, *l.* 6: *read* sēcayati *for* śēcayati, *l.* 19, bā̃ṭula for bā̃ṭulā.

370, *l.* 25: *add*: পুঁতুল « pũtula » *doll* (puttala < putra-la: puttalikā > « Hindi putalī »; MIA *deśī* « poṭṭa » *belly, stomach*, whence Marathi « pōṭ », cf. Bengali পোঁটা « põṭā » *intestines of fish, anything viscid in a lump*; পুঁজ « pũja » *pus, matter from sores or itches* (pūya > *pŭyya > *pujja, *puñja »; from « pŭyya » we have also « *pŭvva, *pivva, *pibba », whence Magahi and Hindi « pīb » *pus*).

372, *l.* 5, *before* পালকী, *add*: MB পাখুড়ী « pākhuḍī » *petal of flower*, cf. MIA *dēśī* « paṁkhuḍi ».

372, *ll.* 9, 10: the word সকড়ি (সকড়ী), সঁকড়ি occurs in Oriya as « saṃkhuḍi ». The aspirate in the Oriya form suggests MIA « saṃkhaḍa- » rather than « saṃkaḍa- < saṃkaṭa (also < saṃ + kṛta-) » as the source. MIA « saṃkhaḍa- » would be from OIA « saṃskṛta- » *fully done* > *fully cooked.* In Oriya the original sense is preserved: *all foods, rice, curries, pāyasa, etc., which are boiled in water, as opposed to being cooked or fried in ghee or oil, and then such food left over on the plate or leaf, and so unclean.* In North India, সঁকড়ি food is called « kaccā » and *ghee*-fried food « pakkā ».

372, *l.* 5 *from bottom*: Cases of denasalization of « -m- > w̃ »: সাতাসে, আটাসে « sātāsē, āṭāsē » *a baby born in the seventh/eighth month* (*sāta-māsiyā, *āṭha-māsiyā in Middle Bengali); so বারাস্যা « bārāsyā » *belonging to the twelve months* (bāraha + māsiyā).

373, *ll.* 11–12: *read* ʃ̇ *for* ʃ.

378, *l.* 13, *after* e.g. *add*: *Pali* « issēra, acchēra < *ĕssaïra, *acchaïra < *essairia, *acchairia < OIA āiśvarya, āścarya ».

386, *l.* 18: *after* « gā̃ṭa » *add*: beside গেঁটে « gē̃ṭa ».

386, *after l.* 27, *add*: In the novel 'Ālālēr Gharēr Dulāl' (published 1858) by Pyari Chand Mitra, a Muslim character named Bāhulya, i.e. Bāhulla (বাহুল্য—-for বাহাউল্লা Bahā'ullāh), speaking in the village *patois* round about Calcutta, says এজ, কেল « ēja, kēla » (for আজ, কাল « āja, kāla »), and these are the expected transformations of MB « āji, kāli » in South Rāḍha Bengali.

387, *after line* 10, *add*: Epenthesis is still an active phonological process in Bengali to the south of Calcutta, and round about Calcutta, e.g. forms like পাইলে < পালিয়ে = পালাইয়া « pāilē < pāliyē = pālāiyā » *having run away;* দাঁইড়ে, দেঁইড়ে < দাঁড়িয়ে = দাঁড়াইয়া « dā̃iṛē, dē̃iṛē < dā̃ṛiyē = dā̃ṛāiyā » *having stood still.* হাইরে, হেইরে < হারিয়ে = হারাইয়া « hāire, hēirē < hāriyē = hārāiyā » *having lost* or *getting lost,* ঘুইরে < ঘুরিয়ে = ঘুরাইয়া « ghuirē < ghuriyē = ghurāiyā » *having swung round,* গইলে < গলিয়ে = গলাইয়া « gailē < galiyē = galāiyā » *having slipped through*, etc.

392, *l.* 19: *read* [ʃ̇oĭttɔ] *for* [ʃoĭttɔ].

395, *l.* 3: cf. also ব'রো, বোরো ধান « ba'rō, bōrō dhāna » *a kind of rice* ('Dēśi-nāma-mālā': varaya = śāli-bhēdē *a kind of rice*; < varaka; *varuka > *barua + ā > *baruā, *bauruā > bōrō:).

395, *l.* 6: আন্ধুয়া, আঁধুয়া « āndhuā, ā̃dhuā » *dark and damp, underground* (andhuka-).

396, *l.* 3, *from the end*: *read* [borp(h)i] *for* [borp(h)ī].

398, *l.* 10 *from bottom, read* *কুড়লি *for the first* কুড়ালি *and* kuṛāli *for* kurāli.

402, *l.* 14, *before* origin, *add*: to their: *l.* 5 *from bottom, read* [ʃɔre ɔ:].

403, *l.* 14, see in this connexion additions to p. 353, *l.* 7 above.

406, *l.* 14, *add* আঢ্য « āḍhya » *a rich man* আড্‌ঢ্যি, আড্ডি « Āḍḍ(h)yi, Āḍḍi » *a surname, Anglicised as 'Auddy'.*

407, *l.* 9: cf. Hindi « banāī » *making charges for jewellery* > Bengali বানী « bānī ».

409, *l.* 21: *add*: MB *sts.* পরতেখ « paratēkha » (as in the 'Caitanya-Bhāgavata' = Skt. pratyakṣa > *parattiakkha).

412, *l.* 22: *after* (vaivāhika), *add*: so বেন, ব্যান < বেয়ান < বেহাইন « bēn, byān [bæ:n] < bēān < bēhāin » *son's or daughter's mother-in-law* (*vaivāhinī); Skt. « jñāna », MB pronunciation « geāna », in New Bengali [gæ:n] (গ্যাঁন).

424, *l.* 6 *from bottom*: *add* MB « -å̊hå̊-, -å̊ẏå̊- » also occur as [ɔĕ]; e.g. গয়না < গহনা « [gɔĕnɑ] < gåhånā » *ornaments, jewels* (grahaṇa-); ময়না « [mɔĕna] < mayanā » *a talking bird, 'mynah'* (madana-). *In l.* 16, *read* [bɦɔ̃ĕʃɑ] *for* [bhɔ̃eʃa].

430, *ll.* 4 *and* 2 *from the end*: [ʃts] (as in [kɔʃtsit] and [dzoik:hɔʃtsɔk:re:]) is pronounced also as [rc͡ʃ] and [cc͡ʃ].

430, *ll.* 26 ff. The tentative transcription in typical East Bengali pronunciation of the first two verses from the Sanskrit 'Mēghadūta' has to be corrected. Things to be specially noted: (*a*) the aspirate [ɦ] becomes [ʔ], the glottal stop, and it changes its place; (*b*) [gɦ, ɟɦ, ḍɦ, dɦ, bɦ], voiced aspirates, have the recursive pronunciation with the glottal stop accompaniment, as [gʔ, dzʔ, ḍʔ, dʔ, bʔ]; (*c*) « śc » becomes « cc » [c͡ʃc͡ʃ] or [rc͡ʃ], not [ʃts]: kaścit = [korc͡ʃit].

438, *l.* 9: *read* § 84 *for* § 86.

440, *l.* 2: *after* (anduka), *add—chain to bind feet of an elephant.*

440, *l.* 21: *read* gå̊ṛ *for* gå̊r; *last line, correct* † *to* ‡.

441, *l.* 3: *The Aspirates.* It should be noted that the aspirate nasals and liquids (« nh, mh, rh, lḥ »: cf. 'Prākṛta-Paiṅgala', Bib. Ind. ed., p. 6) occurred in OB and Early MB, and these became deaspirated in the Late MB stage.

443, *l.* 5 *from bottom*: *read* « **āda̸lā** » *for* « **ādla** ».

448, *after l.* 15, *add new para*:

There is in the Modern Standard Colloquial, a doubling of a consonant in some compounds as well as verb-forms in connexion with a preceding « -i- » vowel: e.g. বছর দুই-তিন > দুত্তিন « bachara̸ dui-tina̸ > duttina̸ » *two or three years*; গোটা দুই-চার > দুচ্চার « gōṭā dui-cāra̸ > duccāra̸ » *about two or four pieces*; following the MB forms করিছে, ধরিছে, চলিছে, etc., « karichē, dharichē, calichē » *is* (*or are*) *doing, holding, going* > Modern Standard Colloquial ক'র্ছে or ক'চ্ছে, ধ'র্ছে or ধ'চ্ছে, চ'ল্ছে « ka'rchē or ka'cchē (ka'ccē), dha'rchē or dha'cchē (dha'ccē), ca'lchē », we have MB জাইছে (যাইছে), খাইছে, ধুইছে, দুহিছে, হইছে, পাইছে « jāichē, khāichē, dhuichē, duhichē, haichē, pāichē » *is going, is eating, is washing, is milking, is happening, is getting* > Standard Colloquial যাচ্ছে, খাচ্ছে, ধুচ্ছে, দুচ্ছে, হ'চ্ছে, পাচ্ছে « jācchē, khācchē, dhucchē, ducchē, ha'cchē, pācchē ». Where there is an « h » in the root as a non-initial in MB, the loss of « i » is usually resisted in Modern Bengali, e.g. MB কহিছে, দুহিছে, গাহিছে, চাহিছে « kahichē, duhichē, gāhichē, cāhichē » *is speaking, is milking, is singing, is asking* in Modern Bengali we have কইছে, দুইছে, গাইছে, চাইছে « kaichē, duichē, gāichē, cāichē » beside ক'চ্ছে দুচ্ছে, গাচ্ছে, চাচ্ছে « ka'cchē, ducchē, gācchē, cācchē » : the forms retaining the -ই- « -i- » would still appear to be more common. We have thus a case of « i+consonant » giving rise to loss of « i », with this loss compensated by doubling the consonant. Is it a case of the ই « i » first changing to « y », and then possibly to the glottal stop « ʔ » as a substitute for the « y », and finally the glottal stop originating in this manner assimilating with the following consonant and doubling it? (Do we see a reverse case of Latin « ct = kt, pt » changing first to « tt » in Vulgar Latin and then this « -tt- » changed to « ʔt- », and finally to « -it » in French—as in the case of Latin « factum, coctum, lactem, septem » first becoming « fatto > fattu, cotto > cottu, latte, sette » and then « fait, lait, cuit, set » (written 'sept', but probably it was « *seit » first)? The colloquial form জাতঃপাত (for জাতিপাত) « jātappāta̸ » *outcasting* for « jāti-pāta » is peculiar:

there might have been intermediate stages like « jāit-pāta > *jāˀt-pāt > *jāta ?pāt > jātappāt ». *See* p. 1026, *and Note on it, below.*

449, *l.* 5: *add* recent *before* foreign, *and put a comma afterwards. After l.* 8, *add*: Other instances of assimilation: « n > m »: মোহন-ভোগ « mōhana-bhōga » *pudding made of semolina, ghee and sugar* > « mō(h)ŏna-bhōga > mōmbhōg »—« mumbhōg » in the Calcutta Colloquial; « ṇḍ > n > ŋ »: ডাণ্ডাগুলি « ḍāṇḍā-guli » *tip-cat (game)*> ডান্‌গুলি, ডাংগুলি « ḍān-guli, ḍāṅguli ».

451, *l.* 22: *correct* pañca *to* pɑñca; *l.* 24, *at the beginning, add*: « -ṛ- » is similarly assimilated to a following [ʃ], as in মাকড়সা « mākaṛasā » *spider*, Calcutta Coll. মাকসা, মাকোসা « mākåsā » [mɑkɔṛʃɑ > mɑkoʃɑ], হাঁড়ীশাল « hā̃ṛiśāla » *room for pots, kitchen* « hā̃iṛśāla » by Epenthesis, then হেঁশেল « hē̃śēla ».

452, *l.* 5, *and l.* 4 *from bottom*: *correct* < *to* >.

452, *l.* 13: The doubling of a consonant before « y, v » in *tss.* (turned in this way to *stss.*) is really a case of *Progressive Assimilation*: e.g. « satya » > [ʃotto], « vākya » > [bakko], « sattva » > [ʃɔttɔ], « dvitva » > [dittɔ], etc. With the « -y- », there was a stage of Epenthesis first: « satya > *saitya > [ʃotto] », etc.

453, *l.* 17: *correct* gh *to* gɦ.

456, *l.* 10: *add*: শালিক, also শালিখ « śālika, sālikha » *a chattering bird, a magpie* (sārikā, MIA *sālikka-); শালুক « śāluka » *a kind of lotus* (śāluka *lotus root or stalk*, MIA *sālukka-).

456, *l.* 14: *correct* kā̃ka *to* hā̃ka.

456, *l.* 16: *add*: বুক « buka » *chest, heart* (bukka < vṛkka *kidney* = Avestan vərəδka).

456, *after l.* 30, *add new lines*:

« ṣk » : বকনা « bakanā » *heifer* (RV.I.164, 5: vatsa baṣkaya *yearling calf*: later Skt. baṣkayaṇī, baṣkayiṇī, also with va-: *a cow with a young calf*: cf. verse by Sonnoka, No.41 in the 'Kavīndra-vacana-samuccaya').

457, *l.* 2: MB (ŚKK) বাঁহুক « bā̃huka », NB বাঁউক, বাঁক « bā̃uka, bā̃ka » *a carrying pole for the shoulder, with a load at each end or wing* (vihaṅgika, *vahaṅgika, Hindi bahaṅgī).

459, *l.* 2: *bring here as the first example* খড়ী *from line* 8.

459, *l.* 12: *add* খোঁপা « khō̃pā », OB « khōmpa- » *hair braided and done into a loose knot* (« kṣupa » *shrub, bush* > « *kṣupya, *khuppa, *khumpa »; also

Ṛgveda I, 84, 8: « kṣumpa » translated as *shrub*, explained by Sāyaṇa following the Nirukta as an « ahicchatraka » *mushroom, a plant rolled up on the ground like a serpent.* Cf. Sindhi « khumb » *mushroom*: semantic change, from shape of mushroom to that of a loose hair-knot.

460, *l.* 8: *add* MB কড়খা « karakhā » *war-song* (« kaṭākṣa » = *angry eye, challenge*; cf. Hindi « karakhā » *battle-song*, « karakhait » *a singer or minstrel in battle*: the Bengali denominative verb কড়কা « karakā » *to rebuke*, may be from কড়খা.

460, *after l.* 8, *add in a new paragraph*: OIA « -kṣy- »: ভেখ, ভেক « bhēk(h)a » *mendicancy, the life of a monk, monk's garb* (bhaikṣya); শিখ « śikha » *a Sikh*, borrowed (?) from Hindi and Panjabi « Sikkh, Sīkh, < *sēkha < MIA *sĕkkha < Skt. śāikṣya » *disciple, pupil.*

461, *l.* 5: *add*: MB অনিমিখ, অনিমেখ « animikha, animēkha » *continually, without a twinkling of the eye* (animēṣa).

462, *l.* 15, *add*: Bengali তাগা « *tāgā* » *a string, an armlet* (from MIA *dēśī* tagga = *sūtra*. But cf. also Hindi dhāgā = *string*, also *strong*).

463, *last two lines.* In the MIA forms for « Vitastā > Vihattha » *the name of the river in the Panjab* = Western Panjabi « Vēhat », Kashmiri « Vyath, Veth », and for « vitasti » *span* « vihatthi », Helmer Smith sees the influence of « hattha < hasta » for the MIA « h ». But « -gh- » in this Bengali form of the word, বিঘৎ « bighat » remains unexplained. Regular forms of OIA « vitasti », with loss of « -t- », occur in some NIA speeches.

468, *l.* 13: *add* so *before* long.

470, *l.* 2 *from bottom*: *correct the semicolon before* পেঁচা *to* >.

471, *l.* 8, *supply, after* jēāca: *woman with first child living*; *l.* 9, *before* etc., *add*: MB আচাভুআ « ācābhuā » (accabbhua-, atyadbhuta-); *after l.* 11, *add as a new paragraph*: OIA « -rc- » > MIA « -cc- », also « -ñc- »: আঁচ « ā̃ca » *heat of flame* (arciḥ); কুঁচি « kūci » *brush* (kūrcikā).

472, *l.* 2 *from bottom*: *read* *es-ské-ti *for* *es-sko-ti.

472, *l.* 26: *before* 'etc.' *at the end of line, add*: *sts.* ছিষ্টি « chiṣṭi » *world* (sṛṣṭi).

473, *l.* 2: *read* *pro + bhu-ské-ti; *l.* 3, *read* *pṛk-ské-ti; *l.* 17, *add at the end*: MB নেউছা, নিছা « nēuchā, nichā » *adorn* (nēvaccha-, nepathya-: there is another word in MB নিছা « nichā », for which see *infra*, p. 551).

473, *after l.* 28, *add*:

The MB root নিছা « nichā » is difficult to explain. It means *to sacrifice* (নিছানি, নিছনি « nichāni, nichani » *to sacrifice, to offer, to propitiate, to offer or to cast something to avert the evil eye, to honour* = Hindi « nichāwar » *sacrifice, offering, money scattered on festive occasions.* It is possibly the 'Atharva-Veda' word « niś-cātaya- » *to scare or drive away,* but we have also « ni-kṣap: ni-kṣapayati < √ kṣap » *to fast, abstain from, do penance* (also « ṇi-kṣip » *to throw away,* to influence it semantically ?).

475, *l.* 13: *read* 'fry' *for* 'try'; *l.* 3 *bottom, correct* † *to* ‡.

478, *after l.* 12, *add new entry*:

ঝক্খি, ঝক্কি « jhakk(h)i » *responsibility* (*failure entailing censure*), cf. MIA *dēśī* « jhakkia, jhinkhia » *censure, upbraiding.*

After l. 20, *add*:

ঝড় « jhaṛȧ » *rain-storm, storm*: cf. MIA *dēśī* « jhaḍi » *pouring or continuous rain.*

479, *l.* 24: ঝাড়—there is the *dēśī* word « jhāḍa » meaning *a thicket of creepers* (latā-gahana): ঝাড় also has an extended sense—*a chandelier of glass* (with many arms, resembling the branches of a tree).

480, *l.* 15: *delete* * *before* dhītā, *and add after* duhitā): (the MIA « dhītā » is derived by some scholars from IE « *√dhē » *to suck* = OIA « √dhā », which is found in the Latin « filius, filia ».)

l. 7 *from bottom*: *read* ঝুঁঝা *for* ঝঁঝা; *l.* 5 *from bottom, read* ঝুটা *for* ঝটা.

482, *l.* 20, *add*: OB জোঙ্গডা, NB জোংড়া « jōṅgaḍā, jōṅṛā » *snail, oyster*; cf. Bhojpuri « ghōṅghā ».

484, *l.* 18: *read* « mard-āmi » *for* « mardāmi »; *l.* 5 *from bottom, delete one* and.

488, *l.* 26: *read* ḍāśa *for* ḍāsȧ.

490, *l.* 2: *add* টেমি, টিমি « ṭēmi, ṭimi » *a tin lamp, burning kerosine* (cf. Bhojpuri « ṭēmi » *soot gathered round a wick,* also *sprout of plant*).

490, *l.* 16: *read* টাট্টু *for* টাট্ট.

493, *l.* 22, *add, at the end*: আঁউঠা, আঁইঠা, আঁইঠুয়া, এঁঠো, এঁটো (by Umlaut) « ā̃uṭhā, ā̃iṭhā, ā̃iṭhuā; ē̃ṭ(h)ō » *uncleared plates or spot after a meal, unclean* (āmṛṣṭa = apariṣkṛta).

495, *l.* 5: *read* ḍiba *for* dimmba.

495, *l.* 18: *after* 'snake', *add*: (ডেঁপুয়া, ডেঁপো « ḍē̃puā > ḍē̃pō » *pert, impertinent,* as in ডেঁপো ছোকরা « *over-smart, impertinent boy*: cf. NB ডেঁপ

«ḍēpå [ḍǣp]» *the young of a snake*; cf. also Bhojpuri «ḍapōr» = «bēwuqf» *foolish*).

497, *l.* 1: পড়িহায় in the ŚKK—we have it as পড়িহাহে = পড়িহাএ.

497, *l.* 15: cf. also হাড় «hāṛå» *bone*, Hindi «haḍḍī = MIA *dēśī* haḍḍa».

497, *l.* 25: *add*, NB নোড় «nōṛå» *an acid fruit* (Averrhoa acida: Skt. lavalī > *lavaḍī).

498, *l.* 15: *read* ডেগ *for* দেগ.

499, *l.* 4: «ḍhibåri» also means *a lamp* (usually *a tin lamp without chimney, burning kerosine*).

500, *l.* 14: *after 'town', add*: Old Slav «gordŭ», Lithuanian «gar̃das».

501, *l.* 14: *add*: বেসাত «besātå» *trade, business, buying and selling* (vāiśya-tva) extended to বেসাতি «besāti», by -i affix; আইহত, আয়্যত, Calcutta Bengali এওৎ «āihata, āyyat; ēōt» *married state of a woman* (avidhavatva: cf. Early Awadhi ahiwātā; Marathi ahēv = avidhavā).

501, *l.* 33: *before* যাঁতা, *add* জাত «jātå» *a religious procession or ceremony, religious or cult songs* (yātrā: cf. yātrā-gāna > jātå-gānå).

502, *l.* 9: *from bottom*: *correct* > *to* <.

502, *l.* 11: *add, at the end*, চিরাতা, চিরেতা «cirātā, cirētā» *a very bitter drug* (OB cirāyita, OIA Kirāta-tikta-); নিমিতা, নিম্‌তা, নিম্‌তে «nimitā, nimåtā, nimtē» *a village name* (nimba-tikta-; cf. the Sanskrit name of the town of Modjopahit in Java: bilva-tikta-).

502, *ll.* 16, 17: *delete* উরুত «urutå» *thigh* (p. 325): see below, p. 503, *l.* 24, and also Addition under p. 504, *l.* 27.

502, *l.* 26: *add* MB ধামাত «dhāmāta» *a religious devotee*, as in the 'Sūnya-Purāṇa' (dharmānta: cf. Early Maithili kāmāt *servant* < karmānta).

502, *l.* 31: *add* তাত «*tātå*» *hot, heat* (tapta); MB ছাতীঅণ «chātīaṇa» dialectal ছাতিয়ান, ছাত্যান, ছাইতান also ছাতিম «chātiyāna, chātyānå, chāitānå, chātimå» *a seven-leaf tree* (sapta-parṇī).

504, *last line, before* মুথা, *add*: MB উরাথ «urātha» *thigh, thigh-bone* > NB উরাত, উরত, উরোত, উরুত «urāta, uratå, urōtå, urutå» (uru+astha, urvastha, as in the 'Śatapatha-Brāhmaṇa'); ভাথী «bhāthī» *bellows*, in Barisal dialect (bhastrā-).

507, *l.* 9: *after* «udhō», add *a fool, an idiot*.

509, *l.* 21, *read* পুঁটী মাছ *for* পুটী মাছ.

510, *l.* 10 *from end*: *add*, *after* « rūpā » *silver*; *and after* rūpya-, *stamped coin, with figure* (= rūpa).

510, *after l.* 21, *add*: OIA « -pn- »: MB সোপ « sōpa » *sleep*, as in the 'Śūnya-Purāṇa', p. 85: সোপ করিয়া উঠিলেন গোসাঞি পত্তুস « sōpa kariyā uṭhilena gōsāñi pattusa » *early in the dawn the Lord got up after having slept* (svapna > MIA soppa, suppa).

513, *l.* 2 *from bottom*: *correct* বেওড়া *to* বেওরা.

513, *l.* 22, *after* (mukula), *add*: cf. Bhojpuri « bawãri—ām-kē bawãri » = Bengali আমের বোল, বউল.

514, *l.* 8: *after* -mr-, *add* *-mbr-.

514, *after l.* 17, *as a separate para*: OIA « -vy- »: the future base ইব « -iba- » (OIA -itavya-, MIA -iavva-, -iabba-).

514, *l.* 29, *add*: But the word is found in MIA as a *dēśī* word — « babbari = kēśa-racanā ».

515, *l.* 5, *read* bhūkhȧ *for* bhukha; *after l.* 23, *add as a separate para*: OIA « -dbh- »: MB আচাভুআ « ācābhuā » (atyadbhuta-); *and then, after that, add the portion from* উভিয়া যাওয়া *to* (ud+$\sqrt{}$bhṛ, bhar) *in ll.* 31–33 (*by mistake entered under* OIA « -rbh- »).

515, *l.* 22: *add at the end*: A form « bhēḍra » is found in OIA lexicons whence MIA « bheḍḍa > (Bengali) bhēḍā, (Nepali) bhēṛō, (Panjabi) bhēṛȧ, (Western Panjabi) ḍhleḍḍ, (Sindhi) bheḍrī ». Bengali « mèḍā » = Hindi « mēṛhā », Sinhalese « mäḍa », from OIA « mēḍhra » (Amara-kōṣa) < Indo-Iranian *maiždhra (whence probably also Skt. « mēṣa », Hindi « mēs, mēh » — « mēḍhra, *maiždhra » probably connected with OIA « mēhati » (R. L. Turner, JRAS, July 1928, p. 667, see also below, p. 555, *ll.* 4, 5, from bottom, where the entry under « mēṛā » is also to be corrected as above).

515, *l.* 25, *add*, *after* (sabhyāgāra): (Nalinikanta Bhattasali in *Ep. Ind.* XVIII, p. 85, derived « sābhāra » from « sambhāra > sabbhāra » *wealth and plenty*.

517, *l.* 13: the word চাউল « cāulȧ » *rice, husked and uncooked rice*, is probably Austric: see Suniti Kumar Chatterji, 'Two New Indo-Aryan Etymologies' in the 'Zeitschrift für Indologie and Iranistik', Leipzig, 1932, pp. 31–40.

519, *l.* 19: *add*: The spellings in the 'Crepar Xaxtrer Orthbhed', « xuoron » = স্বওরন, স্মরণ, « atua » আতুআ, আত্মা, etc., indicate an attempt to represent, in the Portuguese orthography of this work, the nasalized « w̃ » pronunciation of a post-consonantal « -m- ».

520, *l.* 9: *before* MB গোঙাএ, *add*: গুঁই « gũi » *a surname.*

520, *l.* 30: A few more examples of « -m- > -w̃- »—nasalization of « w »: OB পঁউআ « pãuā » *lotus* (MIA *sts.* paduma- = OIA padma-: cf. Bhojpuri paũ-nār = padma-nāla); গোঁআর « gȭāra » *rustic, uncultured, rough* (grāmāgāra); গুঁই « gũi » *a surname* (gōmika, gōmin *owner of cattle, rich farmer*: cf. Candra-gōmin, grammarian of Bengal, *c.* 600 A.D. = NB as in চাঁদ গুঁই Cā̃da Gũi); MB বাঙন « bāṅana = bāw̃ana » *dwarf* (vāmana) : cf. NB বেঁটে-বাঙ্কুরা « bẽṭē-bāṅkurā < *bāṇṭiyā-bāw̃aṅkara < -ākāra- » *short, 'of bantam height', and dwarfish*; *বাওঁণ্ডলিয়া > বাঁউণ্ডুলে' « *bāȭṇḍaliyā > bā̃uṇḍulē » *vagabond, vagrant, homeless, without work* (vāta-maṇḍala-ika: cf. Hindi bawaṇḍar, baũṇḍar *whirlwind, confusion*).

521, *l.* 6: *add* সাতাসে', আটাসে' « sātāsē, āṭāsē < sāta-māsiyā, āṭha-māsiyā » *child born in the seventh or eighth month*; বারাস্যা, বারাসে' « bārāsyā, bārāsē < bāra-māsiyā » *a poem describing the 12 months.*

521, *l.* 11: *before* ছাতিম, *add*: Standard Coll. গোম্‌নে [gomne] *late*, a *sts.*, for গৌণে « gauṇē [goune, gõwne] » (< gāuṇa-).

522, *l.* 11: *add*: খড়ম « kharama » *wooden clogs* (Hindi kharāȭ, Nepali kharāu: *khaḍāw̃a < *khaḍāwa < kaṭṭha-vāua < kāṣṭha-pādukā).

523, *l.* 10: *read* ē̃ *for* ē.

525, *l.* 9 *from bottom*: *read* most *for* all; *l.* 3, *from bottom, correct to* intervocal.

527, *l.* 9: *correct to* বিষ্টুপুরের.

531, *last line*: cf. also *sts.* folk-forms like ভগমান্ « bhagamān » for ভগবান্, *ভগৱান « bhagabān, *bhagawān » (bhagavān); ভাগ্যিমানী « bhāgyimānī » *as a sts. feminine form of* « bhāgyavān ».

532, *l.* 12: ফুল-ম্‌-পেড়ে: cf. Assamese ফুলাম্ কাপোৰ « phulām kāpōr » *cloth with flower embroidery.*

533, *l.* 17: *before* Final..., *add*: Also নায়ক « nāyaka », pronounced commonly as [nɑek]; *l.* 22, *add at the end*: cf. the traditional pronunciation of Sanskrit forms like « Harāya, Yādavāya, Mādhavāya, Kṛṣṇāya » as [ɦɔrɑe, ʒɑdɔbɑe, mɑdɦɔbɑe, kriʃṭɑ̃e] in Vaishnava chanting or singing.

534, *l.* 11 *from bottom*: correct to পক্ব.

535, *l.* 2: *read* (ŏ) *for* (ō̆).

536, *l.* 13 *from bottom*: *read as follows*: at a later time, Early Braj-bhakha in the West as well), to change . . .

541, *l.* 26: before মাল্লে, *add*: নেমন্তন্ন « nemantanna » *invitation to lunch or dinner* (nimantraṇa > *nēmantarna); এথেকে, যাথেকে « ētthēke, jātthēkē » *from this, from what* < « ēra thēkē, ihāra thākiyā; jāra thēkē, jāhāra thākiyā ».

543, *l.* 13, *add*: Faridpur District নৈদ [noid] < *লইদ, র়ইদ < রউদ্দ < রৌদ্র; *l.* 26, *add at the end*: Cf. Assamese « bhārāl = bhā̃ḍā̃r » (bhāṇḍāgāra), « pariyāl » (parivāra *family*), and Hindustani, Bihari *stss.* « daliddar, calittar » (daridra, caritra).

545, *l.* 11: *before* নুন, *add* নোড় « nōṛa » *an acid fruit* (lavalī > *lavaḍī).

548, *l.* 11 *from bottom*: *read* apa-smarati *for* pra-smarati.

548, *l.* 19, *add* আশগঁদ « āśa-gā̃da » *a medicinal plant* (aśva-gandhā); আশ-শেওড়া, শাওড়া « āśa-śāoṛā, -śēoṛā » *a plant* (aśva-sākhōṭa-).

549, *l.* 1: *read* śiṃśapā *for* śiṃsapā.

550, *l.* 9: *read* si *for* sī; *l.* 2 *from bottom*, *read* śatāyuḥ.

550, *add at the bottom*: In order to avoid this pronouncedly dialectal transformation of « s » to « h », which is held in ridicule, sensitive speakers of East Bengal dialects are occasionally found to use artificial forms like শার্মোনিয়ম্ for হারমোনিয়ম্ *harmonium*, শাপটিকট for হাফটিকেট *half-ticket*, শাইকোট for হাইকোর্ট *high-court*, etc., with the idea that it is correct or 'genteel' to say « শ or স » for হ « h ».

551, *l.* 18: cf. also MB বিছুরে « bichurē » for বিসরে « bisarē » *forgets* (vi-smarati) and Bengali মুছি, মুচি « muchi, muci » *earthen crucible* (mūsikā; cf. Early Maithili mūsī, mūsā).

553, *l.* 25: *add*: র‍্যা [ræ:] *furrow line* (Murshidabad: র‍্যা-কানা হ'ল্ছে [ræ-kɑnɑ holc͡ʃhe] *the plough has gone off the straight line* (MIA rēha, OIA rēkhā).

554, *l.* 9: গম « gȧma » *wheat:* possibly there were three forms in spoken OIA, connected with the Persian « gandum » and the various other connected forms in the Iranian speeches (see Paul Horn, 'Grundriss der Neupersischen Etymologie', Strassburg, 1893, p. 209, No. 935), viz. (i) « gōdhūma (as in Sanskrit), (ii) *gēdhūma (whence Hindi gēhū̃), and (iii) *gadhama (whence Oriya gaham, Bengali *gaama > *gȧma > গম gama) ».

555, *l.* 27: *before* কাহন, *add*: MB (ŚKK) আহা « āhā » (āśā).

556, *l.* 9 *from bottom*: *read* bā̃ĭcī *for* bå̃ĭcī.

557, *l.* 10: *read* sāhā *for* sāha; 11, *read* nēhå *for* nēha.

560, *l.* 9: *read* regarded *for* regard: *l.* 12, *read* Saifī *for* Saifi.

563, *l.* 3 *from bottom*: *correct to* syllable.

565: *top.* The Sounds of Old Arabic. Following the analysis of Arabic sounds by W. H. T. Gairdner in his 'Phonetics of Arabic', Oxford University Press, 1925, the table of Arabic sounds given on this page requires some correction:

After the compartment for *Glottal Sounds*, there is to be added another for the *Pharyngal Sounds* of ح [ħ] and ع [ʕ] which have been now properly identified in their articulation. In this Pharyngal Compartment are only two Fricatives, voiceless [ħ = ح] and voiced [ʕ = ع].

566, *l.* 8: Cf. the Indian pronunciation of « āqā » *lord, master, gentleman* as « āgā, āġā » (Āghā).

l. 11: This [tʃ] pronunciation of ك [k] is known as the 'kaškaša' pronunciation in the Arab world (Najd, Hijaz, etc.).

l. 20: *after* Greek, *add*: and Persian, Indian and other foreign. . .

l. 21: *after* « gamma », *add*: Thus we have Arabic جلينوس « Jalīnūs » < Greek « Galēnos », انجيل « injīl » for « euangelion », جرجس « Jirjis » from Greek « Gēorgios », جند « jūnd » for Persian گند « gund », نارجيل « nārjīl » for Persian « nārgīl » = Skt. « nārikēla », پادنجان « bādinjān » for Persian « bādingān » = Skt. « bātiṅgana », etc.

568, *l.* 18, *after* thing, *add*: cf. ضاهر *manifest* = « lahir », رضا *a name* = « rela » in Malay; and in the Malayalam speech of Kerala in South India, رمضان *the Arab month Ramadan*, is pronounced (among the Moplahs) as « Ir'amaḷān' », وضو *ablutions* as « vuḷu », حاضر *present* as « hāḷir », etc.

570, *l.* 8, *read* 'Moghals' *for* Moghals; *and in the Table of Consonants, take* h *from the Semi-vowel to the Fricative Line.*

572, *after l.* 19, *add*: Transformations into Sanskrit and Prakrits of Perso-Arabic (and Turki) words, through popular North Indian pronunciation during the period of the Turki conquest, tenth to thirteenth centuries A.D. (with an artificial, archaistic orthography in some cases) are interesting: e.g.

« śūratrāṇa or suratāṇa, Hammīra, Turuṣka or Turukka, Musallimāṇa, Addahamāṇa, babbarī, Arabbī, Kurāṇa, pāïkka, kammāṇa, nimāja, Khurāsāṇa, masīta, pēyāju, dokkāṇa, kitēba, mulukka, pātisāhī, gālima, Asalāna, Imarāhima = Sulṭān, Amīr, Turk, Musalmān, ʻAbd-ar-Raḥmān, bābrī, Qur'ān, pāïk, kamān, namāz, Khurāsān, masjīd, pyāz, dūkān, kitāb, mulk, pātišāhī, ġālib, Arslān, Ibrāhīm » etc.

575, *l.* 17, *add*: But in « ġalṭān » *wallowing, rolling* = গুল্তান, গুল্তন « gultăn » *chattering, loud talking,* the « -a- » is probably changed to « -u- (or -o-) » through influence of গোল « gōla » *round,* also *noise.*

576, *l.* 7: *read* [tɑ̃bu] *for* [tā̃bu]; *l.* 11, *correct* Hindōstanī *to* Hindōstānī; *l.* 23, *read* ɦab(e)li *for* ɦab(e)i; *l.* 25, *read* হালুয়া *for* হালূয়া; *l.* 26, ɦabʃi *for* ɦabʃi; *and l.* 29: cf. also [saɦn] *courtyard* > « sāna » *stone or cement paving.*

577, *l.* 4 *from end*: *read* রিশবৎ *for* বিশবৎ.

579, *l.* 22: *correct* inām *to* inˤām.

580, *l.* 9: *read* হিন্দু *for* হিঁন্দু; *and l.* 5 *from bottom, before* and, *add*: and আমারী « āmārī » *canopied seat on elephant* (ˤimārī): *l.* 25: *add* ফরাশ, ফরাস « pharāśa, pharāsa » *carpet* (firāš).

581, *l.* 14: *read* corpses *for* corpes.

591, *l.* 16: *correct* 2 *to* 3.

592, *l.* 16: *correct* naɦr *to* nahr; *l.* 25, fiqr *to* fikr.

593, *last line*: *add* In *as the last word.*

595, *l.* 12: *delete* বল্লম, etc. (it is an Indian word).

596: *l.* 19: *add* মায় « māy » *along with, accompanied by, including* (Arabic maˤ, maˤa, *vulgo* maˤe).

597, *l.* 9: *add* শিকদার « śikadāra » *a surname, an official title* (siqq-dār *Officer in charge of a district*). *l.* 23, *add*: Cf. Panjabi « vakhat » (waqt), Gujarati « śōkh » (šauq).

598, *ll.*11–12: *after* Arabic *add* « kausaj < kausag » (Persian); *l.* 32: *after a mistress, add*: cf. Bhojpuri « khāngī », with « g »: another interpretation is that it is from « xānqah » *an establishment for Sufi religious men* > *a woman who visits it.*

599, *l.* 10: *before*, etc., *add* খাসী « khāsī » *a castrated goat* (xassī).

602, *l.* 18: *correct* « šart » to « šarṭ ».

603, *l.* 15: *add*: গোঁড়া « gõṛā » *a blind partisan, an ultra-orthodox person*; গুণ্ডা « guṇḍā » *a ruffian, a paid rough* (Persian « gundah » *army, troops* > Arabicized to « jundah », from I–Ir « vṛnda-ka »).

608, *l.* 5: *add, before* জমী; in Bengali, a nasalized long vowel (-ān, -īn, -ūn > -ā̃, -ī̃, -ū̃) in a final position generally loses the nasalization: গজা « gajā » *a sweetmeat (fried wafer sweetened with syrup, shaped like a tongue)* (gāw-zabān > *gaojawā̃); নিম্‌কী « nimkī » *salted, pertaining to salt* (namkīn, nimakīn); আয়লা-সয়লা « āyalā-sayalā » *effusive friendship* (*among women*), (ahlan-sahlan *welcome*).

608, *l.* 12, *from bottom*: *correct* pĥæ̃ʃad *to* phæ̃ʃɑd.

608, *l.* 16: *add* ফাঁস « phā̃sa » *making public* (fas).

610, *l.* 19: *before* etc. *add* মিদ্যা, মিদ্দে « midyā, middē » *a surname* (mīr-deh = *head of a village*).

610, *l.* 29; *add after* (illat): একলাই, দোলাই « ēka-lāi, dō-lāi » *one-fold, two-fold* > *a piece of cloth tied round a child's head and neck as a loose cloak* (lāʔ = *fold*).

611, *after l.* 11: *add* মোচোরমান « mōcōrmān » (musalmān—through a Bihari folk-form mucunmān).

612, *l.* 23: *add* ছিঁচ্‌কা, ছিঁচ্‌কে, ছিক-চা « chĩcakā, chĩcakē < chik-cā » *a very slender iron rod, to clean* huqqa *tubes or pipes* (sīx-cah).

613, *l.* 5, *from bottom*: *before* হাজির, *add*: নজর [nɔɟʒɔr] *present, offering* (naor).

614, *l.* 2: Also আখেজ « ākhēja » *encroachment* (*over rights of any one*), *enmity, rivalry* (axao, axaz); MB. করধা beside NB করজা, করজ « karadhā, karajā, karaja » *loan* (qarđ, qarz); খিদির « Khidir », as in the place name খিদিরপুর « Khidir-pur » *Kidderpore* (xiđr+pur).

619, *add, at the bottom*: Quite a number of Persian loans have been fully naturalized, and they are looked upon, as pure Indian words: e.g. সরম « sarama » (now-a-days spelt also as শরম « śarama ») *shyness, modesty* (šarm); শক্ত « śakta » *hard, strong* (saxt); সুস্থে « susthē » as in ধীরে-সুস্থে « dhīrē-susthē » = *slowly, in a leisurely manner* (sust); সৌখীন, সখ « saukhīna, sakha » *taste, liking, amateur* (šauq, šauqīn); নির্যস, নির্জস, নির্জোস « nirjasa, nirjōsa » *unmixed, pure* (Skt. nir+jōš *excitement*); and hybrids with « -ḍā or -ṛā » affix, like হিজ্‌ড়া, লাঙ্গড়া or ল্যাঙ্গ্‌ড়া, বেদ্‌ড়া or ব্যাদ্‌ড়া, তগ্‌ড়া or তাগ্‌ড়া « hija-ṛā, lāṅga-ṛā or lxṅga-ṛā,

bedȧ-ṛā or bæḍȧ-ṛā, tag-ṛā, tāg-ṛā » (< hiz *eunuch*, lang *lame*, bad *bad* or *evil*, tag *running*), etc.

620, *l.* 7, *after* West Bengal, *add*: During the sixteenth century and considerable part of the seventeenth century, the Portuguese controlled the Indian seas (Bay of Bengal, the Indian Ocean and Arabian Sea), and Indian maritime trade and commerce were at their mercy. An interesting side-light into the state of affairs is thrown by a treaty between the Portuguese in Goa and Paramānanda, the Raja of Bakla in South Bengal (*el Rei Parmananda, Rei de Bacalaa*), who sent as his emissaries to Goa two men, Ni'amat Khān (*Nematcão*) and Kānu or Ganu Biswās (? = *Gannu Bisuar*)—the latter being the Dewan of the Raja (*Veedor da fazenda do el Rei*). Dom Constanino de Bragança was then Viceroy of Goa. The treaty was executed on 30 April, 1559. The Raja was to give certain trade privileges to the Portuguese, in return for *cartaxes* (passports or naval licences) for four ships of the Raja being permitted annually to visit three ports in the Indian waters, two for Goa, one for Ormuz and one for Malacca. Presents were sent by the Raja to the Portuguese authorities, and there were other terms (see Surendranath Sen; 'Historical Records at Goa', Calcutta Review, May, 1925, pp. 171–194).

For Luso-Bengali literature (Bengali works written by Portuguese *padres* and under Portuguese auspices), see *ante*, Note on *page* 136.

621, *l.* 10: *correct* Collectcd *to* Collected.

623, *l.* 11: *read* তোলো *for* তোলা.

625, *l.* 5: *read* 'coffee' *for* 'caffee'.

643, *l.* 6: *before 'theatre'*, *add*: (also ঠিয়েটার « ṭhiēṭār », commonly in Calcutta cockney, through assimilation with the following cerebral).

MORPHOLOGY

654, *l.* 20: *after* « karata », add রাগত « rāgata » *angry*, *angry-like* (rāga *passion* > *anger*), as in একটু রাগত হইলেন « ekȧṭu rāgata hailenȧ » *he became a little angry.*

656, *l.* 13: *read* ghūrṇ- *for* ghūrn-.

657, *l.* 24: *before* পাখনা, *add* পোনা « pōnā » *fish spawn*, also *children, offspring* as in ছানা-পোনা « chānā-pōnā » (pōta- + -na-).

658, *l.* 4: *read* রাঁধনী *for* রাধনী.

658, *l.* 15: *correct* « vana » *to* « pavana » (OIA « danta-pavana- »—this is a disguised compound: cf. পলাশন, মান্দারন, জাম্বনী « palāśanȧ, māndāranȧ, jāmbanī » *place-names*, from « palāśa-vana, mandāra-vana, jambu-vana > *jāmbaana + -ī »).

658, *after l.* 15, *add*:

(5c) From অনিয়া, অ'নে, ওনে, উনে « -ana- + -iyā > -aniyā, -a'ne, -ōnē, -unē » in the sense of *doer*: দুখ-দিয়নিয়া > দুখ-দিউনে', মিছ-কহনিয়া > মিছ্-কউনে, কান্দনিয়া > কাঁদুনে', etc., « dukha-diyaniyā > dukhȧ-diunē, micha-kahaniyā > michȧ-kaunē, kāndaniyā > kā̃dunē *one who weeps* » etc.

659, *l.* 23: *before* etc., *add* চৌতিশা « cautiśā » *acrostic and alliterative verses, with the 34 consonants* (cau-tīsā < catus-triṃśat-ikā).

661, *l.* 15: *after* of course, *add*:

The source might also be, at least in some cases, OIA « -āyita » meaning *behaviour or nature of*: e.g. বাম্নাই « bāmnāi » (brāhmaṇāyita), চোরাই « cōrāi » (caurāyita).

661, *l.* 19: দোলাই: see also Note on *page* 610, *l.* 29.

661, *l.* 24: *before*, etc., *add* ঝাড়াই « jhāṛāi » *cleaning, cost of cleaning* (ঝাড় « jhāṛȧ < jhāṭa » *brush, shrub > broom-stick*); পোঁছাই « pō̃chāi » *rubbing, mopping* (পোঁছ « pō̃ch » < « pra-uñch »); কামাই « kāmāi » *earning through work > abstention from work* (*with full pay!*) (karma); বোঝাই « bōjhāi » *loading* (bōjha = *load*).

661, *l.* 30: *before* মিঠাই *add*: হাড়াই, ডোমাই « hāṛāi, ḍōmāi » *the uncultured or boorish ways of a Hāḍī, a Ḍōm > riotous behaviour.*

663, *l.* 9, *add at the end*: cf. Assamese « pōwātī ».

663, *l.* 13, *add*: cf. also West Bengali গোড়াইত, গোড়াৎ « gōṛāitȧ, gōṛātȧ » = Magahi « gōṛait » (gōḍa, MIA *dēśī* gŏḍḍa *foot* > gōḍaïta *footman, attendant, watchman*).

664, *l.* 3, Other words with same affix: ঘেরাও « ghērāō » *surrounding* (√ghir, √gher); লাগাও « lāgāō » *attached* (√lāg *be in contact*); মিল- —মিলাও « mil- —milāō » *close unity* (√mil); বিকাও « bikāō » *for selling* (probably < Hindi « bikāū »); কমাও, বাড়াও « kamāō, bāṛāō » *lessening, extending* (kam, √bāṛh); etc.

665, *l.* 11: Other words: বানান « bānānà » *spelling of words*; *building* or *making* (varṇāpana): চিতান, চিতেন « citānà, citenà » *rousing* (*cittā-pana); চাপান « cāpānà » *pressing, attack* (√cāp); ছিটান « chiṭānà » *sprinkling* > ছিটেন « chiṭenà » *off the tangent, irregular* (applied by some Bengali Roman Catholics to Protestants) (√chiṭ); ভাসান « bhāsānà » *floating* (√bhās); খাওয়ান-দাওয়ান « khāōānà-dāōānà » *feasting* (*khādā-pana, *dāpāpana); আগুয়ান « āguānà » *advancing* (agra + -āpana); পাছুয়ান, পেছোন « pāchuānà, pēchonà » *going behind* > back-side (pāch < paścā + -āpana); গোবাড়িয়ান > গোবেড়েন « gō-bāṛiyānà > gō-bēṛēnà » *thrashing with a stick* (*bāṛi*), *as a cow or ox* (gō: gō + bāṛi + -āpana).

665, *l.* 26: *after* (= darśanī); *add* হাঁফানী, হাঁপানি « hā̃phānī, hā̃pāni » *taking deep breath, asthma* (< hā̃ph).

666, *l.* 2, *add*: Cf. also মউনী, মৌনী « maünī, maunī » as in ঘোল-মউনী « ghōlà-maünī » *churning stick* (*to separate whey from cream*) (*mathanikā-); MB মেলানী « mēlānī » *farewell* (√mel = *spread* or *cast away, throw* + -āpanikā).

666, *after l.* 12 *add*:

(14a) আনিয়া, আনে « -āniyā > -ānē: -āna- (*kṛt* suffix) + -iyā (*taddhita*)». An extension of suffix No. (14)—found in a few words in an agentive, attributive or abstract sense, or with implied familiarity or contempt: e.g. লতানে « latānē » *creeper-like* (latā + āniyā); একানে « ēkānē » *singly, all by oneself* (ēka-); EB (Barisal) ঘিয়ের বানানিয়া মিঠাই « ghiyērà bānāniyā miṭhāi » *sweet or pastry made with ghee*; হাঁটানে বেটা « hā̃ṭānē bēṭā » *a stepson*, lit. *a son who comes walking with his step-father, after his widowed mother's remarriage*: among Muslims in parts of South Bengal (√hā̃ṭ + āniyā); যোগানে, জোগানে « jōgānē » *one who supplies* (yōga-), ভোগানে « bhōgānē » *one who causes to suffer* (bhōga-); খেদানে « khēdānē » *one who drives away* (< khēdā *driving*); হারাণে, পরাণে « Hārāṇē; Parāṇē » *contemptuous forms of names like* Hārāṇà-candra, Parāṇà-candra or Prāṇa-kṛṣṇa). Cf. also the forms like সুখ-জাগানিয়া, ঘুম-ভাঙ্গানিয়া « sukhà-jāgāniyā, ghumà-bhāṅgāniyā » (used by Rabindranath Tagore); কাঁদানে' < কান্দানিয়া গ্যাস « kā̃dānē gyās » = *tear-gas*. These forms would be slightly archaic for modern Standard Colloquial. There has been a merging of « -ăna- » and « -āna- », owing to phonetic decay.

666, Section 410, *add*: আমানী « āmānī », also pronounced আওঁয়ানি « āw̃āni » *water in which boiled rice has been soaked for the night, slightly fermented* (ācāma-pānīya); ধারানি « dhārāni » *water or liquid which trickles or flows down* (dhārā); ছেরানি « chērāni » *watery excrement* (cf. Gujarati chēr, chērāṇṭō, *ibid.*).

667, *ll.* 9, 10, 11: আমিনী, আমিনি: this word really means *a follower of a deity or a teacher, a member of a sect, an attendant, a servant* (in the last sense it is found as « āmanajka » in the Maithili 'Varṇa-ratnākara', p. 406; from OIA « āmnāya, āmnāyin, āmnāyika »).

667, *l.* 31: *add*: ফাজলাম, -লামি « phājalāma, -mi » *cheekiness, behaving like a learned man* (Pers. fāzil); ডেঁপোম, ডেঁপোমি « ḍẽpōma, -mi » *over-smart or cheeky behaviour* (< ḍẽpa *young of snake*, ḍẽpuā > ḍẽpō *over-smart boy*).

670: *read* rūpālī for rupāli *in l.* 7, *and* rūpuli *for* rupuli *in l.* 8.

670, *l.* 9: *add*: Other instances of this « -āla » and its extension « -ālī »: নামাল « nāmāla jami » *low land* (nām, √nam); মিশাল, মিশালি, মিশেলি, মিশিলি « miśāla, miśāli, miśēli, miśili » *mixture, mixing* (√miś); ঝাঁঝাল « jhā̃jhāla » *with a strong or pungent flavour*; জমকাল « jamakāla » *gorgeous* (« jamak », as in « jā̃k-jamak » *gorgeousness*); ঠাকুরাল, -লি « ṭhākurāla, -li » *behaviour like a god or a prince* (ṭhākura); বড়াল « baṛāla » *a big man > a surname* (*Dēśī* baḍḍā *big, great*); ভিজাল, ভেজাল « bhijāla, bhējāla » *watered > adulterated* (bhijā *moistened*); গাঁধাল, গাঁদাল « gā̃d(h)āla » *a strong smelling plant, the leaves of which are used as a drug* (gandha-; also gandha-mādala); হোঁড়ল, হাঁড়াল, হাঁড়িয়াল > হেঁড়েল « hō̃ṛala, hā̃ṛāla, hā̃ṛiyāla > hē̃ṛēla » *a hyena* (*Dēśī* ? cf. Hindi huṇḍār *hyena*; the basic word may be « haṇḍā, or haṇḍī » *a big earthen pot*, and connected with it are many other words like « huṇḍā » *an idiot*, « huṇḍi » *insurance* (= *money put in a pot: money sent in business transactions*, etc.; cf. also হোঁদল « hō̃dala » *fat, pot-bellied*); আলাল « ālāla » *rich man* (? Perso-Arabic 'alā' = *superior*; also explained to mean *without son or child*—a + lāl = *without son*, which is doubtful); দুলাল « dulāla » *a pet child, a darling* (dulā < dullaha < durlabha-, also = *bridegroom*); in the Sundarbans, to the South of Calcutta, we have বাটাল « bāṭāla » *way-laying, waiting hidden for prey* (bāṭa < vartman); মাঠাল « māṭhāla » as in মাঠাল দেওয়া *driving, e.g. deer along fields or open* *spaces* (māṭhă *field*), গাছাল « gāchālă » *waiting for* shikār *from the top of a tree* (gāchă), শিঙ্গাল, শিঙ্গেল « siṅgālă > śiṅgēlă » *horned*, as in কাঠ-শিঙ্গেল « kāṭhă-śiṅgēlă » *with dry horns*, so চাম-শিঙ্গেল « cāmă-śiṅgēlă » *with velvety horns* (for deer); MB সুতালি « sutāli » *function as a charioteer* (in Giris Chandra Ghosh), on the model of নাগরালী, নাগরালি « nāgarālī » *the way of a gallant or a lover*, ঠাকুরালি « ṭhākurāli » *the way of a God*, etc.

In OIA, this affix « -āla » was both a primary (*kṛt*) and a secondary (*taddhita*) affix, and both have become indistinguishable in Bengali.

670, *after l.* 21, *add*: Also Maimansingh মৈষাল « maisāla » *buffalo-herd* (mahiṣa-pāla); Sundarbans Bengali মউলা, মউলো, beside মাওয়ালি < *মহুআলী « maulā, maulō, māoāli < mahuālī » *a collector of honey* (*madhu-la-, ? madhu-pālika); NB গেঁজেল < গাঁজিয়াল « gẽjēlă < gā̃jiyāla » *a hashish addict* (gañjikā-pāla).

Note also some old Brahman surnames from names of villages: কাঞ্জিলাল « Kāñjilālă » (Skt. Kāñji-bilva-pāla > MIA kañji-illa-āla), পুষিলাল « Pusilālă » (< Pōṣala- or Poṣila-pāla), মোতিলাল, মতিলাল « Mōtilāl » (?Mauktika-illa-pāla, *Mottia-illa-āla), ঘোষাল « Ghōṣālă » (< Ghōṣa-pāla).

672, *l.* 17: *read* রাঁধনী *for the first* রাঁধুনি.

673, *l.* 2: *read* বষ্টুমী *for* বষ্টুমী.

676, *after* § 423, *add new section*:

(28a) -ইতা « -itā ». The source of this « -itā, -tā » is not clear. See below, p. 692, No. (48), and add in that connexion নালিতা > নাল্‌তে « nālitā > nā'ltē » *leaves of the jute plant used as greens, bitter in taste* (cf. kirāta-tikta > OB cirāyita, NB cirātā, cirētā: *a bitter herb* < ?nāla + tikta- > nālitā; but found in the 'Prākṛta-Paiṅgala' as nālica-gaccha); চালিতা, চাল্‌তা, চা'ল্‌তে « cālitā, cālătā, cā'ltē » *an acid fruit*; পাল্‌তে মাদার « pāl'tē mādără » from « *pālitā-mandāra » *a plant*; বালতো, বালদো < বালিতুয়া, *বালিতা + উআ « bālătō, bālădō < *bālitā-uā » *the fronds of the coconut* (?); তল্‌তা, তল্‌দা « tală-tā, talădā » *a kind of very slender bamboo, for making umbrella-handles*, etc.

676, *after* § 424, *add new section*:

(29a) ইয়ান > এন « -iyāna > -ēnă »; extension ইয়ানিয়া, আনে «-iyāniyā, -ānē ».

This adjectival affix indicates connexion: from OIA « -iyā (or -ikā-) » *plus* a generalized adjectival « -ana ». Examples পূবেন « pūbēnȧ » *easterly, eastern (as a breeze)* (pūba < pūrva, *pūbiyāna); ন'লেন < নলিয়ান « nå'lēnȧ < naliyānȧ » *new, as of date-palm molasses* (navaliya- + ana); গ'ড়েন < গড়িয়ান « ga'ṛēnȧ < gaṛiyānȧ » *sloping* (*Dēśi* gaḍḍa *to roll*); মিঠেন « miṭhēnȧ » *sweet, sweetish* (miṣṭa-). Words in this « -iyāna, -ēna » are comparatively few in number. (But Bengali পড়িয়ান > প'ড়েন « paṛiyāna > pa'ṛēnȧ » *woof* (from OIA pratitāna); Jessore Bengali কাতিয়ান > কা'ত্যেন « kātiyānȧ > kā'tyenȧ » *belonging to the month of Kārttika* (OB and Assamese কাতী, কাতি « kātī », OIA « kārttika »: used for rice, winds and storms). The word খতিয়ান « khatiyānȧ » *estimate, statement of loss or gain*, either from Perso-Arabic « xatt » *writing, letter, accounts*, or from Skt. « kṣati *loss* = khyati + iyāna ».

There is a Maithili affix « -āin », adjectival, as in « dudhāin, pitarāin, kasāin, kaṭhāin, telāin, ichāin », etc., = *milky, brazen, astringent, wooden > tasteless, oily, like prawns* (ichā, icā), etc., but it is different in origin.

677, *l.* 18, *add*: A few words in « -ēlā » are connected with the suffix: « -ita + -illa-, -alla > -ielā, -ēlā »: e.g. সুরেলা « surēlā » *with fine tune* (sura < svara), ঝামেলা « jhāmēlā » *trouble, tumult* (jhamma, jhampa), বনেলা « banēlā » *wild* (vana), হিমেল « himēlȧ » *cool, icy* (himȧ-), আধেলা > আধ্লা « ādhēlā, ādhȧlā » *half, half-pice* (ardha-), etc.

677, *last line*: *read* pleonastically *for* peonastically.

679, *l.* 13: *the source of* দেরখো « dērȧkhō » is OIA « dīpa-vṛkṣa- ».

682, *l.* 13: *read* ḍholla *for* dholla; *l.* 20: before পুঁটকে, *add*: মেচ্‌কো, মেচ্‌কা in মেচ্‌কো or মেচ্‌কা ফের « mecȧkā, mecȧkō » in « mēckō phērȧ » *a strong knot, a complication < a knot in a jute rope* (< মেচা « mēcā » *jute* in tracts to the south of Calcutta). Cf. also place name মেচাদা « Mēcādā (< mēcā + daha) ».

682, *bottom of page*: So কান্‌কো « kānȧkō » *fish gills* (kāna < karṇa). The word আন্‌কো, also আন্‌কা « ānȧkō, ānȧkā » *strange, unknown, odd,* suggests « āna < anya + -kuā », but there is another form আন্‌খো, আনখা « ānȧkhō, ānȧkhā », with which we may compare Hindi « anōkhā, anaukhā » *strange, new, rare, not seen before* (< an-avēkṣā- *not seeing or testing before* + -uā in Bengali).

683, *after l.* 23, *add*:

A pleonastic or approximative use of an extended form of this « **-ka** » affix, « -aka, -ēka », is found in forms like কতক, কতেক « kataka, katēka » *a little, a certain amount* (কত « kata » *how much?*); so যতেক, ততেক « jatēka, tatēka » (< যত jata, তত tata); ক্ষণেক « kṣaṇēka [khɔnek] » *for a short while* (kṣaṇa); দিনেক « dinēka » *about a day* (dina); গোটা দশেক টাকা « gōṭā-daśēka ṭākā » *about ten rupees* (daśa), খান তিনেক বই « khāna-tinēka baī » *some three books*, গোটা আষ্টেক টাকা « gōṭā-āṣṭēka ṭākā » *about eight rupees*, etc.

684, § 434. The source of ঘামাচী « ghāmācī » would appear to be OIA « gharma-carcikā », by haplology of « -ca- ». We have in Assamese ঘরচীয়া « gharaciyā » *domestic* (ghara + -cca + -iā), কুন্ধুচ « kundhuca » *hateful, repulsive* (kabandha-), দাবচা « dābacā » *a kind of grass* (darbha-), বানচ « bānaca » *cost of making a thing* (varṇa-tya-), etc.; Bengali বাহিচ, বাইচ, বা'চ « bāhica, bāica, bā'ca » *boat-race* beside Assamese বৈচা, বাইচা « baicā, bāicā » *boatman*, may be connected with « vahitra *boat, ship* > vāhitrya > *-bāhicca », but « bāha » *to row a boat*, বাহী « bāhī » *a rower* cannot be dismissed; Bengali ছোঁয়াচ « chõāca » *contagion* (√chõ *to touch*) may also show the same affix.

684, *after* § 434, *add*:

(39a) -চ, -আঁচ « -ca, -ãca- », extended to চি, আচি « -ci,-āci ». This is from OIA « apatya » *offspring*: e.g. বেঙ্গাচি « beṅgācī » *tadpole* (বেঙ্গ « bēṅga < vyaṅga » *frog* + « apatya- > avacca- »); জেয়াঁচ « jēyãca » *woman with her baby living* (jīvitāpatyā); মড়ুঞ্চে < মড়ঞ্চিয়া « ma'ṛuñcē, maṛañciyā » as in মড়ুঞ্চে পোয়াতি « ma'ṛuñcē pōāti » *a mother whose children die early* (mṛtāpatyā-).

(A « -c- ; -ñc- » affix, in a few words like কেরাঞ্চি « keranci » *a hackney carriage* (cf. Hindi kirāyā *carriage-fare*), ঘোড়াঞ্চি « ghōṛāñci » *a high stool to reach things* (ghōṛā), বালাম্‌চি « bālāmci » *horse-hair* (bāla), remains unexplained.)

685, *after l.* 6, *add*: গুমোট, গুমট « gumōṭa = gumaṭa » *sultry weather, hot and moist without breeze* (grīṣma > gimha, *gumha + vṛtta); Sundarbans Bengali প'ট < পইট « pa'ṭa = pōṭ, paiṭa » *narrow forest track for deer* (pada-vṛtta, *paya-aṭṭa); চ'ট < চইট « ca'ṭa, caiṭa » *movement of deer* (cara-vṛtta ?), আট < আইট

« āṭa̍, āīṭa̍ » *high land in the jungle with evidence of previous human occupation* (?); NB লোপাট « lōpāṭa » *obliteration, removal, destruction* (lōpa-).

686, *after l.* 21, *add*: This affix « -ṭā, -ṭi, -ṭī » now behaves like an independent word, meaning *one piece, a single item*: e.g. এটা, ওটা, সেটা « ēṭā, ōṭā, sēṭā » *this piece, that piece, the other one*; উপরের-টা, নীচের-টা « uparēra̍-ṭā, nīcēra̍-ṭā » *the one at the top, the one at the bottom,* এ বছরের-টা « ē bacharēra̍-ṭā » *the one belonging to this year,* কাছের-টি « kāchēra̍-ṭi » *the nice little one near at hand*, etc.

686, *bottom*: *add*: বখাটে, বকাটে « bakhāṭē, bakāṭē » *a boy gone astray* (Bengali বখা, বকা « bakhā, bakā » = Hindi « bahak-nā » *to go wild* or *astray* < « bahakka: vah-akka + vṛtta-ika-āka > bakhāṭiyā »).

688, *l.* 5: *correct* <, *before the word* সাপুড়ে, *to*, >; *read* sāpåṛiyā *for* sāpåriyā.

688, *l.* 9: With this is to be connected হাটুরে < হাট+র+ইআ « hāṭurē < hāṭa-ra iā » *a man of the bazaar*; কাঠুরে < কাঠ+র+ইআ « kāṭhurē < kāṭha-ra-iā » *a wood-cutter*; ঢাকুরে < ঢাকরিয়া « ḍhākurē < ḍhāka-ra-iā » *a drummer* (?): cf. ঢাকুরিয়া « Dhākuriyā » *name of a place in South Calcutta*, etc.

688, *l.* 25: *add*: আগাড়ী, পিছাড়ী « āgāṛī, pichāṛī » *before, after* (agra + vāṭa-ika, paścā + pṛṣṭha > picha + vāṭa-ika); আঁকড়া « ā̃ka̍ṛā » *to embrace, to grasp with both arms* (aṅka-vāṭa-: cf. Old Bengali aṅka-wālī *embrace*, Old Hindi ãkwārī = aṅka-pālikā); চাপড়া « cāpa̍ṛā » *to pat, to slap* (cappa *to press* + vāṭa); সাবাড়, সাবড়া « sābāṛa̍, sāba̍ṛā » *finishing, to finish completely* (? sarva-vāṭa-).

692, *l.* 2: *after* « ēōta̍ », *add*: cf. Early Awadhi as in Tulasīdāsa « ahiwātā »; *and at the end of the line, add*: বেসাত, বেসাতি « bēsāta̍, bēsāti » *trade, buying and selling* (vaisya-tva).

692, *l.* 12: These words also show the same affix: কাস্তে < *কাসিতিয়া « kāsa̍tē < *kāsitiyā » *sickle* (OB Sarvānanda « kāsīa̍, Pāṇini *Uṇādi* « kāśū, kāsū » *a spear or lance*, + patrikā); কোঁস্তা < *কোঁচতা « kō̃sa̍tā < *kō̃catā » *a small broom* (Bengali kuci *brush* < kūrcikā *fine brush* + patra-); মেচতা, মেছতা, মেস্তা « mēca̍tā, mēcha̍tā, mēsa̍tā » *a plant like the hibiscus, from fibres of which ropes are made* (cf. Bengali মেচা « mēcā » *jute* + patra ?).

697, *l.* 6 *from bottom, add*: « ugra-rūpa » *exceedingly fierce*, Pali « kalla-rūpa < kalya-rūpa » *exceedingly blessed* ('Sutta-nipāta', Nālaka-sutta 2). The word « kāma-rūpa > kāuru » in Assamese has retained something of its original sense as *whimsical, awry, ugly*: in slang Bengali কেঙুরে (কেউঁরে) « kēṅurē = kēũrē » (< *kāw̃aruiyā) meaning *crooked, ugly,* possibly carries on a pejorative sense of the word. Cf. also MB ঝামরু « jhāma-ru » *pale, dried up* (jhāma-rūpa).

The English word *kangaroo* has fallen in line with the above in Bengali. Cf. also Bihari (Magahi, Maithil) « but-rū » *child, baby > silly person,* from Turki « buta » *child*+Indian affix « -rū ».

697: *Above affix* No. (54), *add*:

(53a) রোল, রুল « rōla, rula ». This rare affix, found in Sanskrit in a few compounded words as « rōla », occurs in the names of a few insects and plants. There are, e.g. the MB words উতরোল « utarōla » *loud noise, strong, forceful, full of trepidation, anxious, eager* (*sts.* from ut+rōla: *loud-sounding*) and উভরোল « ubharōla » *too much noise, high or loud noise, neglect* (MIA. ubbha < ūrdhva + rōla), where we have the same word, which is on the way to becoming an affix, like « rūpa » giving « -rū, -ru, -ur ». The exact sense is not clear—it may mean *making a noise or buzzing sound, or sounding like, or resembling* (√ru), but that does not explain all the words. Examples: ভিমরুল, ভিংরুল « bhimarula, bhiṃrula » *a hornet* (Skt. bhṛṅga-rōla *a wasp*); কাঁকরোল « kā̃ka-rōla » *a kind of fruit* (? kaṅka), < also *an abscess in the arm-pit* (< kaṅkha < kakṣa); জামরুল « jāmarula » *star-apple* (jambu); আমরুল « āmarula » *a small shrub, with leaves of an acid taste* (āmra); MB., South Bengali বাঘরোল « bāgha-rōla, bāgha-rola » *hyena*; বুরুল« burula » *a finger-joint, a third of a finger-length* (?). Cf. also place names like সুরুল « Surula », তিরোল « Tirōla »; MB মারুলি « māruli » *road, path.*

R.L. Turner in his 'Comparative Dictionary of the Indo-Aryan Languages' does not postulate « rōla » as a likely basis for these compounds, and some of the words he explains differently. NB পারুল, জারুল « pārula, jārula » *names of trees,* are from « pāḍali, *jāḍali = Skt. pāṭali-, jāṭali- ».

699, *l.* 5 *from bottom*: *read* ঝুপসা *for the second* ঝাপসা.

699, *l.* 28, *before* ঝাপসা, *add*: কোহাসা > কোয়াসা, কুহাসা « kōhāsā > kōāsā, kuhāsā » *fog,* beside Early Bengali কুয়া « kuā » Magahi « kuhā » *fog*; ধুমসা

« dhumasā », feminine ধুমসী « dhumasī » *bulky, ungainly* (Bengali ধুমা, ধুমো « dhumā, dhumō », Assamese ধুমা « dhumā » *big, bulky, ungainly*).

701, *l.* 21, *add*: cf. Hindi « duhrānā » *to repeat.*

702, *l.* 4 *from bottom*: *read* thānī *for* thanī.

703, *l.* 1: *correct to* Perso-Arabic.

704, *before* No. (4), *add*:

(3a) জাত « jāta »: a Sanskrit form, which in Bengali pronunciation as [ɟʒɑto], represents both Sanskrit « jāta, yāta » *born, gone*, is now quite common: e.g. পকেটজাত « pākēṭ-jāta » *put inside one's pocket*, খাতা-জাত « khātā-jāta » *entered in a book*, অভিধান-জাত শব্দ « abhidhāna-jāta śabda » *word entered in a dictionary.*

705, *before Affix* No. (5), *add*:

(4a) তঃ « -taḥ », also তো, ত « -to, -ta »: this Sanskrit affix, pronounced in Bengali as [to], is found with both *ts.* and *tbh.* as well as foreign words, in the sense of *according to, owing to, because of*: e.g. ধর্মতঃ, বস্তুতঃ, ন্যায়তঃ, জ্ঞানতঃ, আইনতঃ « dharma-taḥ, bastu-taḥ, nyāya-taḥ, jñāna-taḥ, āīna-taḥ (*according to the law*: Persian āīn) »; so মুখ্যতঃ, গৌণতঃ « mukhya-taḥ, gauṇataḥ » *primarily, secondarily.*

705, *before* (7), *add*:

(6a) ত্র « -tra » > ত্তর « -ttara », উত্তর « -uttara ».

This is found in a few words meaning *land set apart for a religious purpose.* The source of it is the Sanskrit « -trā », as in « Gūrjara-trā » *the land settled in by the Gūrjara people* > « Gujjaratta > Gujarāt ». We had first ব্রহ্মত্রা « brahma-trā » *land in which Brahmans were settled*, and this in Bengali pronunciation became ব্রহ্মত্তর « bramhōttara » which was written as ব্রহ্মোত্তর, as if made up of ব্রহ্ম+উত্তর, and it got a modified sense of *land without rental donated to a Brahman.* By extension of this form and sense, we have দেবত্র > দেবোত্তর « debatra > debōttara » *land dedicated to a god or his temple*, and পীরোত্তর « pīrōttara » *land dedicated in the name of a Pīr or Muslim saint.*

706, *under* (9) ময়, *add*: It is likely that in the locative sense, as in দেশময় « deśa-maya » *throughout the land*, the affix is partly based on the NIA locative suffix derived from « madhya », noted *infra*, p. 751.

706, *before last line, add*:

(12) স্থ « -stha ».

467a. Following Skt. forms like দেশস্থ « dēśa-stha » *remaining in the land*, সভাস্থ « sabhā-stha » *present in the assembly*, মধ্যস্থ « *madhya-stha* » *remaining in the middle* > *arbitrator*, etc., the compounded « -stha » has come to be used as an affix with *tbh*., and foreign words, in the sense of *occurring at*, *present in*, etc.: e.g. কলিকাতাস্থ « Kalikātā-stha » *of Calcutta*, *from Calcutta*, *staying at Calcutta*; লড়াইস্থ সংবাদদাতা « laṛāi-stha saṁbād-dātā » *war-correspondent*; কর্ণওয়ালিস-ষ্ট্রীটস্থ দোকান « Karṇawālis-sṭrīṭa-stha dōkān » *shop in Cornwallis Street*, etc.

706: There is frequently a free use of some of the common Sanskrit suffixes, even with foreign words: e.g. adjectival « -ya », as in চার্জ < English *charge* + ya » = চার্জ্য, চার্য্য « cārj-ya ; cāryya », falling in line with « kāryya, dhāryya », etc., and meaning *chargeable* (cf. in the Will of Raja Satrughna-dēva Dhavaladēva of Dhalbhum Raj, 11 May 1905—উক্ত চব্বিশ হাজার টাকা আমার ধলভূম জমিদারীর উপর চার্য্য অর্থাৎ দায়-সংযোগ হইবে); না পার্য্যমানে « nā pāryyamānē » *if one is not able* (Bengali √pār *to be able*), colloquially « nā pārjimānē, nā pājjimānē »; affix « -itā, -ita », as in Arabic « nikāh » +Sanskrit « -itā » = নিকাহিতা « nikāhitā » (as in legal documents—তস্য নিকাহিতা বিবি « tasya nikāhitā bibi » *his wife legally married in the nikāh form*, in imitation of বিবাহিতা = Skt. vivāhitā), etc.

710, *l*. 28, *add*: cf. Early Awadhi « asaṅkā » *fear* (Tulasī Rāmāyaṇa : « asa bicāri tumha tajahu asaṅkā » *thinking thus, you abandon fear*).

711, *bottom, below last line, add*: cf. Early Maithili « nir-āpana » *not one's own* (nir+āpana : purukha nir-āpana capala-mati: Vidyāpati): also Bengali নির্ঝঞ্ঝাট « nir-jhañjhāṭa » *without any trouble* (jhañjhāṭa). The prefix « nir- » is also found with foreign words: e.g. « nira-josu » in Early Awadhi (nir+ Persian jōs), Bengali নির্জস, নিজ্জস « nir-jasa, nijjasa » *pure, unmixed*; « nir+ Persian dam » *breath* > নির্দম, নিদ্দম « nir-dam, niddam » *uninterrupted, severe*.

712, *Add at the beginning*:

(5a) পাতি, পাত « pāti-, pāt- ».

473a. This word, in the sense of *small*, occurs with a number of terms, like পাতি-কুয়া or পাত্‌কুও, পাত্‌কো « pāti-kuā, pāt-kuō, pāt-kō » *a small* *well* (as opposed to an ইঁদারা « īdārā » *a large masonry well* < indrāgāra), পাতি-শিয়াল « pāti-śiyālȧ » *small jackal*, পাতি-লেবু « pāti-lēbu » *a kind of tiny lemon (as opposed to other kinds)*, পাতি-হাঁস « pāti-hā̃sȧ » *duck (as opposed to* রাজহাঁস « rāja-hā̃sȧ = *goose)*, পাতি-ভাঁড় « pāti-bhā̃ṛȧ » *small earthen cup*, পাতি- or পাত-মৌড় « pāti-, pāt-mauṛȧ » *an ornament for the head, generally of pith and tinsel* (< mukuṭa), পাতি-কাক « pāti-kākȧ » *crow (as opposed to* দাঁড়-কাক « dā̃ṛȧ-kākȧ » *jack-daw)*, পাতি-নেড়ে « pāti-nēṛē » '*a shaveling*', *small shaven-headed one* = *Mohammedan of the lower castes (a term of abuse)*, etc. The form occurs in East Bengal as পেতি « peti », as in পেতি-কৌআ « pēti-kauā » *crow*, পেতি-মেকুর « pēti-mekurȧ » *kitten*. The source seems to be OIA « patra- » *leaf*, diminutive « patrikā », MIA « pattia » *thin, not thick* (cf. « patra-la- = পাতলা pātȧlā » *thin*). The French « *petit* [pəti, pti] » *small* has been suggested by some as the source of this form, but it is exceedingly unlikely, despite the fact of the presence of the French in Bengal (at Chandernagore), and noting the East Bengali form « pēti » presenting an unexpected vowel in the « -ē- » (the East Bengali form, however, seems to be a borrowing from Standard Bengali, with irregular alteration of the vowel: but cf. মেদি beside মাদী, below, under p. 714).

712, *l.* 12: *after* (< vēlā); 'sts', *add*: cf. Hindi « subēr », also « sukāl » *early, in the morning*, beside « kubēr » *evening*, and (« bikāl » *evening*, « vikālikā > biyārī, byārī » *evening meal*).

712, *l.* 13: *correct* « nābȧlȧkȧ » *to* « nābālȧkȧ ».

713, *under* (5): cf. বদভ্যাস « badabhyāsȧ », sandhi-form for « bad+abhyāsa ». Also বদনাম, বদনামী « bad-nām, bad-nāmī » *bad reputation*.

Under (3): না-দান « nā-dān » *not knowing, ignorant* > না-দান-ইয়া « nā-dān-iyā » *foolish*, in contempt নাদান্যে, নেদানে, ন্যাদানে « nādānyē, nēdānē, nyādānē [= nædane] » *ignorant (for a school teacher)*.

714, *after line* 4, *add*: (8) নর « nar » and মদ্দা « maddā », and (9) মাদী « mādī » or মেদি « mēdi », male and female prefixes < Persian « nar » and « mard », and « mādah » (+Indian affix « -in, -ī »): cf. Maithil « mēdin » (< māda-in-i), Bengali « mēdī > mēdi »: e.g. নর-হাতী « narȧ-hātī » *male* or *bull elephant*, মাদী-হাতী « mādī-hātī » *cow elephant*, মেদি-শিয়াল « mēdi-śiyālȧ » *vixen, she-fox*, মদ্দা-গণ্ডার « maddā gaṇḍārȧ » *male rhinoceros*, etc.

720, *ll.* 8, 9: *delete*: বৎসহারা গাভী « batsa-hārā gābhī » *a cow which has lost her calf. In l.* 11, *read* form *for* from.

724, *l.* 10: *correct* oblique *to* genitive.

724, *l.* 12: In Maithili, we have for the nominative of the reflexive pronoun « apanahi, apanåi, apanē » from « appaṇehi = *atmanēbhiḥ ». Cf. East Bengali (Dacca, etc.) nominative আপনে « āpånē » (for Standard Bengali আপনি « āpåni »), from « *appaṇa-hi »; so MIA « amhahi < OIA asmābhiḥ » = MB আহ্মে = আম্‌হে « āmhē », MIA « amhi < OIA asmē » = MB আহ্মি, আম্‌হি « amhi », both of which fell together as later MB and NB আমি « āmi ».

724, *l.* 19: *after* Bihari speeches, *add*: Cf. also Awadhi (as in Lakhimpuri) « -ai », nominative and accusative plural, as in « barsai, kitābai, bajārai » (Baburam Saksena in the JASB, 1922, p. 311), and Old Oriya as in the inscription of Narasiṁha-dēva IV (*c.* A.D. 1396) has also « -ai < *-ahi » which later became « -ē », as in forms like « nāekaṅ-kai, kīlā-kai, hātha-rai » from earlier « *nāekaṅ-kahi, kīla-kahi, hātha-rahi » (*see* 'The People, Language and Culture of Orissa', being the Ārtavallabha Mahānti Lectures for 1964 by Suniti Kumar Chatterji, Orissa Sahitya Akademi, Bhubaneswar 1966, p. 34).

726, *l.* 9: « kājaṇa kāraṇa » should be explained as « kāja, na kāraṇa », as in Caryā 26 also, = *neither the deed* (*effect*, kārya), *nor the cause* (kāraṇa), as the commentary explains (kārya-kāraṇa-rahita-tvāt).

728, *l.* 23: *after* genitive, *add*: মানুষের দিগে, মানুষের দিগকে « mānuṣērå-digē, mānuṣērå-digakē ».

731, *ll.* 11, 13: *read* professors *for* scholars ; *and in last line but two, put an* '*' *before* মানুষদি.

733, *l.* 5: *read* rājå-nåitik.

734, *l.* 16: *after* « tōharā-sabhå- », *delete* '*we, ye*', *and add*: also « hamarā-lōkani-, tōharā-lōkani- »: these forms in « -sabhå, -lōkani » are not now used in Maithili in the nominative, but only in the oblique, with post-positions added, e.g. « hamarā-sabhå-kē » *our*, « tōharā-lōkani-mẽ » *among you people*, etc.

734, *l.* 6, *before* In MB, *add*: In Padre Manoel da Assumpçam's 'Bengali Grammar' (Dacca Bhawal dialect, *c.* 1730), we have as plural nominative forms like « tahana, oana, xeara » < তাহান tāhāna (tāna), ওহান, ওআন « ō(h)āna » and সেহা-রা « sēhārā = sē-rā »: cf. Calcutta *patois* তানারা, ওনারা, এনারা « tānārā, ōnārā, ēnārā » *they, those people, these people.*

734, *l.* 29: in South Bengal (as in the 'Nīla-darpaṇ' of Dinabandhu Mitra) we have forms like সাহেব-গা-র « sāhēbå-gā-rå » *of the Sahibs* fairly, frequently.

738, *l.* 21: *read* word *for* work.

739, *after line* 9, *add new para*:

In the language of the law courts, we find some artificial forms for the plural with the Persian affixes « -ān, -hā » and the Perso-Arabic affix « -āt » (the « hā » is changed to « hā-y » through the influence of the *izāfat* affix « -i »): e.g. বুজুর্গান্ « bujurgān » *elders* (buzurg-ān), সাহেবান্ « sāhēb-ān » *gentlemen*, বাবুআন্ « bābu-ān » *gentlemen*, উকিলান্ « ukilān » *pleaders* (wakīl-ān); প্রজাহায় « prajā-hāy » *tenants*, কুঠিহায় « kuṭhi-hāy » *offices, establishments*, আমলাহায় « āmålā-hāy » *officers of the court*, আপিস-হায় « āpis-hāy » *offices*; কাগজাৎ « kāgaj-ātå » *papers, documents*, দলিলাৎ « dalīl-ātå » *documents*; মেওয়াহ > মেওয়াজাৎ « mēwāh > mēwāj-āt » *fruits, crops*, বাগাৎ « bāg-āt < bāg » *gardens* (bāg), অজুহাৎ « ajuh-āt » (wajuh-āt) *reasons, grounds, excuses*, etc.

740, *l.* 7 *from bottom*: *read*: a form of Māgadhī.

741, *l.* 9: *read* *ṭhā̃wi *for* thā̃wi; *l.* 12, *add after* NB: so Assamese « gādhaï » (< *gaddahi, gaddahē, gardabhaḥ), « lātāï » (*ts.* latā + -i); *in l.* 24, *read p.* 1 *for p.* 2.

744, *l.* 6: *read* « gōru-ē » *for* « gōṛu-ē ».

745, *l.* 2: *read* « -ānām » for « -anām ».

745, *l.* 3, *after 'through fear', add*: « bhukhēn, piyāsēn » *through hunger, through thirst.*

751, *add as a new paragraph, after l.* 16:

In dialectal Bengali, as in Sylhet, there is a locative affix in « -ō, -å »; e.g. ঘরো, ঘর « gharō, gharå » *in the house* (LSI, V, I, p. 225). This would seem to be based on a MIA « *gharaha » where « -ha » is the OIA affix « *-dha », of a locative character, which is found in Sanskrit as « -ha » as in « i-ha (cf. Prakrit i-dha), ku-ha, sa-ha (cf. Vedic sadha) » and which seems to have been extended to the noun also. (This « -dha » seems to be connected with the other locative affix « -dhi », discussed before at p. 745, and has cognate forms in the Latin « in-de », Slav « kŭ-de »: cf. Thumb, 'Handbuch des Sanskrit', Heidelberg, 1905, § 407).

751, *l.* 8 *from bottom*: *read* an unsolved problem.

752, *l.* 17: This early weakening and loss of the vowel « -a » in the final syllable of the word is noticeable in the speech of Gujarat from the first century A.D. So, in the case of the numerals: « dvādaśa, trayōdaśa, caturdaśa, pañcadaśa, ṣōḍaśa, saptadaśa, aṣṭādaśa » became first « *bāra-sə, tērasə, caüddasə, pannarasə, sōḷasə, saṭṭarasə, aṭṭhārasə » and after that, the final syllable in these modified forms as « -asə > -as » dropped off, so that in Gujarati (and Rajasthani) these ultimately became « bār, tēr, cōd, panar, sōḷ, satar, aḍhār » (and not « bārah, tērah, caudah, pandrah, sōlah, satrah, aṭhārah » as in Hindi and other languages). So also OIA « caliṣyāmi > = MIA callissaṁ » *pre-Gujarati and Rajasthani « *cālisā̃, cālisə », whence now « cālis ».

755, *l.* 5: *after* genitive, *add*: It is seen that in Early Awadhi, « -kara » and « -kēra » are used side by side, as if they were the same affix, only the metre deciding which form to use (e.g.: « saba-kara saṁsaya aru agyānū; manda mahīpanha-kara abhimānū; Bhṛgupati-kēri garaba-garuāī; sura-munibaranha-kēri kadarāī; Siya-kēra sōca Janaka-pachitāwā, rāninha-kēra dāruna-dukha-dāwā »).

756, *l.* 9: *after* word, *add*: G. A. Grierson quotes: « karaṇḍē mālā-kṛtē (Mahāvastu II, p. 245), udyāna-kṛtā āsanā (pl.), rāja-kṛtyam udyānam ». In Early Awadhi, we have as a literary survival or renewal: « Lachi-mana dīkha Umā-kṛta bēkhā, cakita bhayē bhrama hṛdaya bisēkhā ».

Last line but three: *read* puruṣāṇām.

759, *l.* 12: the affix in Assamese seems to be সা «-sā »: cf. also the genitive form « tōmasā-rå » and the locative « tōmasā-tå » in Early Assamese.

763, *l.* 1: *after* explains, *add*: There is another case of the ablative in Caryā 27: « raanahu sahajē kahēi », where « raanahu = ratnāt »; as the commentary explains—« sadguru-vacana-tattva-ratna-prabhāvāt sa mayi sahajānan-daṃ kathayati ».

763, *l.* 21: Other examples of the « -ta » affix for the ablative: MB (as in the ŚKK) জলত উঠিলী রাহী « jala-ta uṭhilī Rāhī » *Radhika got up from the water*; Early Awadhi (Tulasī-dāsa) « mīna dīna janu jala-te kārhē » *like helpless fish, when they are dragged from the water.*

768, *l.* 3: *add*: The use of the conjunctive *having done* in this sense of a post-position is found in Early MIA: e.g. Pali « kin ti katvā = kim iti kṛtvā » = Bengali কি করিয়া « ki kariyā » *by what means?* « hatthē karitvā pecca vekhheyya » *tests with his hands*; « hattha-gatam katvā » *taking in hand*; « sata-sahassaṃ katvā » *in hundreds of thousands.*

769: *under* (10) চাহিয়া, চেয়ে: *add, in line* 7: « jībana cāhi jaubana baṛa raṅga » ('Pada-Kalpa-taru', Vidyāpati) *youth is much gayer than life*; Early Maithil (Vidyāpati), « apana bacana je pratipālaï, sē baṛa saba-hu cāhi » *he who fulfils his own promise is greater than all*: Early Awadhi, Malik Muhammad Jāyasī, « Lanka cāhi ū̃ca gaḍha » *a fortress higher than Laṅkā*; « ēka ēka cāhi ēka ēka balī » *each one was stronger than every other one.*

772: *under Post-position* No. (26), বই baï. My friend the late Professor Sailendranath Mitra, of the Department of Pali in Calcutta University, drew my attention to the use of « bahiddhā » in Pali, with the ablative, to mean *apart from, outside of*: e.g. « itō bahiddhā samaṇō 'pi n'atthi » *outside of this, there is no monk* (Mahāparinibbāṇa-sutta, V, 27). The use of « bahiḥ, bahirdhā (= bahiḥ+dhā) », with the ablative as well as genitive, to denote outside, occurred in OIA (cf. Speijer, 'Vedische und Sanskrit-syntax', §§ 88, 89, 90). The source of the Bengali post-position বই, বহি, বহী « baï, bahi, bahī » would thus be the OIA, « bahiḥ », and not « vyatīta » as suggested in the text.

772, *after* (26), *l.* 14, *add*:

(26a) বাগে « bāgē » *in the direction of, towards*: from OIA « varga: MIA vaggahi > bāgē »: e.g. ঐ বাগে যাও « ōi bāgē jāō » *go that way.*

(26b) বাড়ি « bāṛi » *a stick, with a stick, with any implement that is handy*: e.g. লাঠির বাড়ি « lāṭhirā bāṛi » *with a stick*, জুতার বাড়ি « jutārā bāṛi » *with shoes*; মারয়ে পিঁড়ার বাড়ি, কোণে বসি' কান্দি « māraye pĩṛā-ra bāṛi, kōṇē basi' kāndi » *he hits me with a squatting board, I weep sitting in a corner* (Bhārat-candra Rāya Guṇākar, c. 1750). বাড়ি « bāṛi » appears to be from OIA « vṛta > vaṭa > vāṭa » *surrounding hedge, palings of wood or stick, barrier, bar, big stick*, diminutive « vāṭikā > bāḍi » *stick, cane.*

774, *after l.* 30, *add*: In Early Awadhi (as in the RCM of Tulasī-dāsa), we have « sana » frequently enough: e.g. « baiṭhē parama-prasanna kṛpālȧ, kahata anuja-sana kathā rasāla » *the all-gracious merciful One sat, speaking about pleasing things with his younger brother*; « jānahu muni tumha mōra subhāū: jana-sana kabahū ki karaū durāū » *O Sage, you know my habit: do I ever behave badly with men?* « ewam-astu muni-sana kahēu kṛpā-sindhu Raghunātha » '*So be it*': *with the Sage spoke the Lord of Raghu, the Sea of Mercy*, etc.

775, *l.* 2: In Murshidabad district we have the forms সাঁথে, সাঁতে « sãthē, sãtē », which may be from a nasalized « satthahi > *santhahi ».

775, *after l.* 22, *add*: The MB form হনে « hanē » given above shows change of an « -nt- » to « -n- » instead of to « -t- »: here we have to assume an analogy of the change, in the Verb Indicative Present third pers. plural, of the affix « -nti » to a « -n- » in Bengali, through the imposition or influence of the pronominal forms. (See below, under *Verb*, Affixes for the Present Tense Third Person.)

In Apabhraṃśa we have « huntō, huntē » which is from « √bhū- —bhavant- ». This affix of Bengali, « hante, haite », etc., has been wrongly connected with the MIA « hiṃtō », which is from locative « -hiṃ » + « -taḥ > -tō ».

775, *l.* 29: an atrophied form like « sēti » from « -sant- » for the ablative occurs also in Early Awadhi.

776, *after l.* 29, *add*: We have in Early Awadhi (both Malik Muhammad Jāyasī and Tulasī-dāsa) « huta, huti, hutẽ, hutē » as a post-position for the ablative, from « bhavant- »: e.g. (Jāyasī) « uṭhē puhumi-huti » *he rose up from the ground*; « ōhi-huta dēkhai pāēu darasa gosāĩ-kēra » *through him I could obtain a sight of the Lord*; (Tulasi) « bacana-hutẽ yaha jagata-mō-kīrati pragaṭa āhi » *through the word, my glory is become manifest in this world*; « prēma-hutē dōu-kahā dīnhā Alakha milāya » *through love he brought the two to meet the Unseen*; etc.

777, *l.* 20, *add:* We have also মায় « māy » *along with, together with, with*, from Perso-Arabic « maʕ », in expressions like মূল্য মায় ডাকমাশুল দশ টাকা « mūlya māyȧ ḍākȧ-māśulȧ daśȧ ṭākā » *the price is ten rupees, with postal charges*, স্বামী-স্ত্রী মায় শিশু « swāmī-strī māyȧ śiśu » *husband and wife, together with the child*; মায় জুতা, মায় জুতা-শুদ্ধ « māya jutā, māya jutā-śuddha » *with shoes on*; চামড়ার ব্যাগ, মায় সোনার কাজ « cāmaṛāra byāga, māya sōnāra kāja » *a bag of leather, with gold work*; etc.

778, *l*. 13: In East Maimansingh, we have equivalents of this « -ṭā > -ḍā » with dental « -t- »: e.g. এইতা « ēi-tā » *this piece*, beside এইডা « ēi-ḍā », এইতান « ēi-tā-n » *these*. We have this « -tā » also among the Haijong people, who were till recently Tibeto-Burman (Boḍo) speakers. Is this due to Tibeto-Burmese influence ?

778, *last line, bottom*. In Chinese, particularly in the very much phonetically decayed language of North China, the addition of these enclitic descriptives is a linguistic necessity: Ancient Chinese « *ˎñźi 'nźyen » *two men* becomes in the Modern Peking language « ˎəɹ 'ɹən », in the Suchow language « `ñi ◡ñɛn », and in the Canton language « -yi, $_1$yan »; but owing to widespread phonetic decay and levelling, particularly in the Peking speech, an expression like « ˎəɹ 'ɹən » will not be understood when spoken (although the two Chinese characters will be fully understood all over China), and Peking dialect must use the enclitic word « k'ou » *mouth*, to fortify the word for *man* and to prevent ambiguity: e.g. « ˎəɹ k'ou 'ɹən » = *two mouth* (or *piece*) *man*.

781, *l*. 4: Also cf. expressions like সবটুকু(ন) « saba-ṭuku(n) » *all, the little all, the entire tiny bit or portion*; এতটুকু(ন) « èta-ṭuku(n) » *such a small portion, this little bit*, intensive এত্তটুকু(ন) « ètta-ṭuku(n) » *these very tiny bits or portions*.

781, *add at the end*: (7) ছড়া « chaṛā » (with longish, flexible articles, e.g. এক ছড়া কলা « èka-chaṛā kalā » *a (small) bunch of bananas*, কলা-ছড়া « kalā-chaṛā » *the little banana bunch*; এক-ছড়া মালা « èka-chaṛā mālā » *one (piece of) garland or wreath of flowers*; এক-ছড়া হার « èka-chaṛā hāra » *a necklace*, etc.: ছড়, ছড়া, ছড়ি « chaṛa, chaṛā, chaṛi » means *a stick*: of *dēśī* origin.

(There is another ছড়, ছড়ি « chaṛa, chaṛi » *hide or skin of an animal* which can be compared with a *dēśī* « chavaḍī < *chavaḍa » *skin*, and still another ছড়, ছড়া « chaṛa, chaṛā » *drop, lustration*, also *verse, couplet*.)

790, *l*. 14: *correct to* Wackernagel.

791, *after l*. 13, *add*:

Ferdinand de Saussure proposed « *k_2sek_1s—*kṣakṣ » as the immediate source of the Indian forms: « kṣakṣ > cha-, ṣaṣ; *kṣaẓ-daśa > ṣō-ḍaśa;

$^{*}k_2sek_1stos$ > chaṭṭha ». (See 'Recueil des Publications Scientifiques de F. de Saussure', Geneva, 1922, pp. 435–439.)

792, *under* 'Eight'. Padre Manoel da Assumpçam gives as the Dacca form « axt » = আষ্ট « āṣṭa », a *sts.* form.

793, *l.* 17, *after* Assamese *add*: Already « bāraha > bāra », with loss of « -h- », occurs in the SKK as বার « bāra », probably pronounced [bɑ:rɔ:].

794, *l.* 13, *add*: Padre Assumpçam in his 'Vocabulary', gives only « bix » = বিশ for *twenty*.

795, *under 'The Thirties'*, *l.* 32. In Assumpçam's 'Vocabulary', we have only the old *tbh.* form তীস, তীশ as « tix », without the added or restored « -r- », and the numbers for the thirties also do not show « -r- ».

800, *l.* 15: *read* « śõ » *for* « so ».

801, *ll.* 13, 14: *correct to*: The Sinhalese forms « dahas > dās » *thousand* (*adjective*) and « dahasa > dāsa, dāha » *1,000* (*substantive*), would seem to be better explained as. . .

801, *l.* 18: *after* assumption *add*: Padre Assumpçam in his 'Vocabulary' has given only « dox xo » = দশ শ' « daśa śa » *ten hundred* for *1,000*, and not the Persian loan « hazār » as expected. The Old Indo-Aryan « sahasra » gave « sahassa > *sahaṃsa », which is found in Early NIA (e.g. Panjabi, Hindi), and we have it also preserved in Kashmiri as « sās ». Possibly the name of the Bihar town *Sassaram* is really « Sahas-rām = Sahasra-rāma ».

801, *l.* 21: A MIA form for « sahasra » seems to have been « sahaṃsa » (beside « sahassa »), and this nasalized form occurs as « sahãsa » in Early Western Hindi and in Early Panjabi. An old spelling of the place-name 'Sassaram' or 'Sahasram' in Bihar is 'Sahansram'.

801: *bottom, add*: The *tss* অযুত « ayuta » *10,000* and নিযুত « niyuta » *one million* were sought to be used by serious or scientific literary writers, but they did not catch on. We have লাখ « lākha » or লক্ষ « lakṣa » *100,000*, and দশ লাখ or দশ লক্ষ « daśa lākha, lakṣa » is the usual Bengali word for *one million*. The Sanskrit term অব্জ « abja » was also used occasionally for *100 millions*.

The Indian « krōḍa = kōṭi » has been borrowed in Modern Persian as « karūr », but there it means *500,000*.

802, *l.* 11, *add at the end*: There is also the word সিকি « siki », সিকা « sikā » *a quarter, a silver coin equal to the fourth of a rupee.* The word occurs dialectally as « suki, sukā », and is apparently the same word as the Hind. « sūkā ». Platts derives « sūkā » from « sa-pāda-ka » *with a quarter* ('Hindustani Dictionary'). It may be that here we have the influence of the MIA « sikka » (*see* supra, pp. 194–195) or the Perso-Arabic « sikkah » *coin*, in connexion with the « -k- » consonant (as well as the « -i- » vowel, in the Bengali form).

805, *after l.* 17, *add*:

In Bengali, the words মেঝো, মেজো, সেঝো, সেজো « mēj(h)ō, sēj(h)ō » *second, third* are used in mentioning brothers in order. In compounds like বড়োদাদা « baṛō-dādā », মেজোদাদা « mējō-dādā », সেজোদাদা « sējō-dādā = *first, second, third, elder brother*, contracted forms are common—বড়্দা, মেজ্দা, সেজ্দা « baṛ-dā, mez-dā, śez-dā ». মেঝো « mējhō » is from « mājhuā » < « madhya + -uka + -āka ». The form সেজো « sējō » is difficult to explain: the « s- » may have come to displace the « t- » in তেজ, তিয়জ « tēja, tiaja » as above, through the influence of the Persian « sih » *three*: « sih, seh + Indiana -ja », on the basis of মাঝুয়া > মেঝো, may have given this form. In Dacca Bengali we have সাইঝ্যা, সাউঝুআ « sāijhyā, sāujhuā, sāijhuā ». But a MIA word « sajjhila- » *younger brother* (No. 13094 in R. L. Turner's 'Comparative Dictionary of the Indo-Aryan Languages'), presupposed from the actual Prakrit words « sajjhil(l)aga, sajjilaga » *brother, sister*, beside NIA forms like Maithil « sā̃jhil », Awadhi and Hindi « sañjhil », Nepali « sā(h)ilō *third* (*elder*) *brother in a family*, and Oriya « sāna-mājhiā » *ibid, third brother in a family of four*, would suggest in a basic form in MIA a disguised compound, « saṇha, *sanna » *small* (< OIA « ślakṣṇa » *small, thin, tender, gentle*, whence Hindi « nanhā ») + «*majjhilla, *majjhima » *middle*, as the source or model of the various NIA words—a possibility accepted by Turner.

811, *l.* 17: *read* मुँहि *for* मँह.

817, *l.* 23: In Modern Bengali, for the nominative, the form তু « tu » (rather than তুই « tui ») is fairly common in the speech of the village people in West Bengali districts, like Birbhum, Burdwan and Bankura particularly.

818, *l.* 31. Cf. the Bengali expression তুই-তো-কারী « tui-tō-kāri (karā) = Hindustani tu-taī karnā » *to address people in a familiar or vulgar way* (with « tui » and « tō » instead of « tumi, tōmā-, or āpani, āpanā »), which is exactly like the French *tu-toiyer*, and English *thou-ing and thee-ing*.

819, *l.* 22: also Early Assamese তযু « taju-tazu » *thy.*

821: *In the Table, under Old Plural, Oblique, read* তাঁ *for* তা ; *under New Plural, Nominative, read* তা(হা)রা , *and oblique* তা(হা)দের; *and in connexion with what has been said in l.* 8 *in* § 555, *note*: the form « sa-kaḥ » actually occurs in OIA (Rig-Veda, Śatapatha Brāhmaṇa, etc.): see below, note on p. 993.

823, *l.* 13 *from bottom*: *read* তাঁ *for* তা .

824, *l.* 5: Cf. Early Assamese দেবে ন জানন্ত তাঙ্ক (= Bengali তাঁ-কে), কেনে জানোঁ আমী « dēbē na jānanta tāṅka (= Bengali tā̃-kē), kēnē jānõ āmī ? » *the Gods do not know him, how could we know?*

825, *l.* 17: *read* possesses *for* possess.

828, *l.* 10: *read* tamȧ-rā-rȧ *for* tāmȧ-ra-rȧ.

829, *l.* 2 in § 566: *delete comma after* « ē-ta »; *l.* 5 *read*: base « *tō- ».

832, *l.* 3 *from bottom*: *read* in the Shahbazgarhi Aśōkan.

833, *l.* 1, *before* would, *add*: (Cf. Pali feminine genitive forms « tissa, imissa »).

835, *l.* 7, *read* উহা *for* ঊহা ; *in the Table, under Oblique of Old Plural, read* ওহাঁ *for* ওহা .

839: *read* (F) *for* (D) *before the heading* THE RELATIVE PRONOUN; *and in the Table, under Oblique of Double Plural, read* যাঁহাদের for যা(হা)দের.

840, *l.* 6: « ya-kaḥ » as the source of যে « jē » occurs in OIA, like « sakaḥ » the source of সে « se »: *see supra*, note on p. 821, and *infra* on p. 993.

844, *l.* 10: The source of NB কই « kaï » *where?* is Indo-European « *qʷodhi » (whence OIA « *kadhi » , Greek « pothi » and MIA « kahi »).

845, *l.* 4. The source of « kēha, kēhō, kēo, kēu » , etc., may be OIA « kaḥ > kē+uta > *ke(h)ua ».

851, *l.* 1: (« ahā̃ » is used with superiors also—only Śrōtriya Brahmans restrict it to equals, or use it to a less frequent extent).

857, *l.* 26. The expressions দেবো অখন, দেবো'খন, যাবে'অখন, etc., occur in Jessore dialect in an attenuated form as in দেবোয়্যানে, যাবেয়্যানে « dēbō-ænē, dzābē-ænē » *I shall give, he will go* (*in due time*): « -ænē < ɔkhɔnē »

860, *add at the end*: There are two adverbial forms which occur in the Braja-buli speech of Middle Bengali literature—জনি, জনু « jani, janu » *as if, like, verily* (< yat+nu ?), and জিন « jina » used as a negative particle (mostly with imperative verbs) = *not* (< yat+na ?).

861, *l.* 10. *Themes.* An inadvertent mistake. Themes are the stems of verb roots, made by adding a vowel, « ĕ/ŏ », to which formative affixes were added; and the syllable like « -o-, -nu-, -so-, -to-, -sko-, -dho- », etc., were in Indo-European inflexions which modified the meaning of the root—the nature of the action denoted by it, its 'Aspect'. These syllables were known as « vikaraṇas » to the Sanskrit grammarians; and on their basis (when they were added to the root), the Sanskrit grammarians made an independent classification of Verb Roots in the Conjugation into the *Ten Gaṇas,* or classes—e.g. « bhū, ad, hu, dīv, su, tud, rudh, tan, krī, cur », taking each of these roots as labels for each of these *Gaṇas.*

861, *l.* 14: *read* *-n- *for* -n-.

862, *l.* 3: *delete* themes or; *and below, in Table, put down the word* affix *for* theme.

862, *l.* 4, *read* dīv-ya-ti *for* div-ya-ti.

863, *l.* 3 *below the Table*: *correct to* Suffix vowels.

867, *l.* 3 *from bottom*: *read* cár-i-tav-ā̱i̱ *for* car-i-tav-ā̱i̱.

868, *l.* 25: *correct 'themes' to 'Vikaraṇas'.*

868, *last line* : *Correct as follows :*
calāmi > OB., MB. calȭ ; *calyatē > *calīaĩ > caliē, calĩ.

869, *l.* 12 *from bottom*: *read* Noun *for* Voun.

871, *l.* 15: *read* seem *for* seen.

873, *l.* 12, *read* es-ské-ti *for* es-sko-ti; *l.* 15, *read* খুঁজ for খুঁজ; *l.* 24, *read* ঽবস *for* ঽবর.

874, *l.* 5: *read* lāj *for* āj; *last line, read* Bengali.

875, *l.* 12: *read* es-ské-ti; *l.* 14, *read* pró+bhu-ské-ti.

882, *l.* 22: *read* vyākhyāna *for* vyyākhāna.

884, *l.* 16: *read* দাগা for the second দাগ.

885: *heading line*: *read* COMPOUNDED AND SUFFIXED ROOTS.

885, *l.* 6: But cf. Caryā 7: « hēri sē Kānha, niaḍi Jiṇa-ura baṭṭai » '*look here, Kānha, the city of the Buddha* (*Jina-pura*) *is near.*

889, *l.* 10. An old instance of this extension of the root by « -l- » (> MIA -alla-) affix is বোল « bōl = MIA bolla », which appears to be from OIA « brū » + « -a-l-a > -alla- ». The unextended form « brū » occurred in OB and MB as « bu » (beside the extended form « bōl, bul »: e.g. MB (ŚKK) বুইল « bu(y)ila » *spoke* (past base—« bru-ta + ila > *buailla > buila »), beside বুলিল « bulila (= bolla + illa) » which is from the standardized form বোল « bōl ». « bulila », however, is less common as a new standardized form than the old derivative « bu(y)ila » in the ŚKK, where « bulila » occurs only 18 times, as against « bu(y)ila » 83 times, an old survival. Cf. in MB old survivals like « kaïla (ka̯ila), sut-ila » besides standardized « kar-il-a, su-ila », and Bhojpuri « kail, dhail, sutạl » besides « kar-al, dhar-al, sō-al ». In the SKK, « bul » *speak* as a root occurs 95 times, and « bol » 116 times (there is another root « bul » *to wandẹr about* which is found 19 times). So similarly we have « bhrama + -alla, -ulla > bhōl, bhul » *to forget*.

898, *ll.* 18–19: The dative-accusative with the post-position occurs in OB: e.g. Caryā 12, « matiẽ ṭhākura-ka parinivittā = matyā prajñāpāramitânubuddhyā ṭhakuram iti saṅklēśârōpita-cittam parinirvvāṇârōpitaṃ kṛtam », according to the Commentary. *l.* 3 *from bottom*: *read* like *for* ike.

900, *l.* 12: *read* labh-ē-ta *for* labh-ī-ta.

901, *l.* 3: *read* NB *for* MB.

901, *l.* 27. In NB, in optative forms with যেন « yēna-jēna = [ɟʒæno] », the conjunction যেন may be omitted: e.g. দেখো, ছেলেটা (যেন) বাইরে না যায়, ঠিক সময়ে (যেন) প'ড়তে বসে « dēkhō, chēlēṭā (jēna) bāirē nā jāy, ṭhik samayē (jēna) pa'ṛtē basē » *you will see (that) the boy does not go out, (and that) he sits down to read at the proper time.* Here we have the inception of the use of the old indicative present of NIA for the 'aorist' of the Hindustani: « xudā karē ki wŏh ā jāy » *May God grant that he arrives = may arrive.*

904, *l.* 5: *read* « -aü » : « kar-aü ».

907, *l.* 10, *add*: The affix in the form of « -ũt », however, is actually found in S.-W. Bengali: চলুঁৎ « calũt », etc.

908, *l.* 15: *read* later *for* latter.

909, *l.* 15, *add*: The form « gā » (earlier form « gai, gaĕ ») is also optionally added in Maithili to emphasize the future (cf. Grierson, 'Maithili Grammar', pp. 136–137). *l.* 4 *from bottom* (= *Heading Line*): *read as* (1) Passive Indicative.

917, *l.* 27: *after* Birbhum, *add*: and part of Murshidabad.

918, *l.* 3: *after* p. 266: *add*: also in Kandi (Murshidabad) আমরা খেয়েই « āmȧrā khēyēi » *we habitually eat* (slightly emphatic), lit. *it is eaten by us*, beside আমরা খাই « āmȧrā khāi » *we eat*.

919, *l.* 15, *after* ŚKK *add*: (,) and also in Krittivāsa 'Rāmāyaṇa' (Uttara-kāṇḍa).

923, *l.* 19: already the analytical passive with « √jā » appears to have been established in MIA by the ninth century A.D. (as shown by Baburam Saksena: e.g. « vēḍhiuṃ jāi » *is encompassed*, « vilihiuṃ jāi » *is painted*, as in the 'Karpūra-mañjarī').

924, *l.* 18: *read* lålāṭå *for* lålātå-.

924, *l.* 24: Cf. also « tē nidhanaṃ gacchanti » *they are killed* (with « √gam = √yā > jā »: 'Nalōpākhyāna' in the Mahābhārata), « tē darśanam yanti » *they are seen* (also in the Mahābhārata).

930, *l.* 28: *after* are, *add*: (distinction between singular and plural in the verb is now lost in NB, and the inflexions are the same for both the numbers).

931, *l.* 14: *before* puchami, *add*: khēlahũ, dēhũ, lēhũ (12); *l.* 15: *delete* dehũ lehũ (8); *l.* 16: Muhammad Shahidullah's emendation « biharahũ swacchandē » (for MS. reading « birahū̃ ī cchandrē ») is acceptable.

932, *l.* 7: *read* থোয়োঁ *for* থোয়ো; *l.* 11, *read* পারোঁ *for* পারো.

934: *after l.* 22, *delete lines* 23, 24, 25, 26, 27, 28, 29; *also l.* 32, page 934, *and* 935, *top line—the sentence*, The nasalization . . . form.

935, *ll.* 11–14: The forms for the first person in NB, dialectal « calō̃ » = Standard « cali » (for both singular and plural), have different origins, which was first pointed out by Dr. Muhammad Shahidullah and further substantiated by S. K. Chatterji (*see* Shahidullah's article in the VSPdP, Bengali Year 1337, No. 2, pp. 82–94, and observations on the same by S. K. Chatterji, *ibid.*, pp. 95–98).

The remarkable thing is that while the OB and MB the *Singular* form for the Verb in the Indicative Present First Person originated from the OIA *singular* (e.g. « karōmi > karami > karama > -karō̃ », which is still preserved in dialectal Bengali and in Assamese and elsewhere in NIA), the corresponding form for the First Person *Plural originated from a Passive Construction* (e.g. « asmābhiḥ kriyatē » in place of « vayaṃ kurmaḥ »: « asmābhiḥ kriyatē > MIA amhehi kariyyati > amhahi karīadi, karīai > OB āmhē karīai > MB ām(b)hē kariē, karī > NB āmi kari »: the NB form was extended to the singular also, and supplanted « karõ », at least in the Standard Speech). So the « -i- » affix for the First Person in the Verb Simple Present is really for MB « -i, -ī, īē, -iyē, -iai ». How is it that the Passive Form came to be established for the First Person Plural, Present Tense, remains unexplained: possibly being in the Passive, it was a polite form. There is no analogy from Oriya—there the distinction between Singular and Plural is preserved: Oriya « mu cālẽ, cāli » (the Bengali root « √cal » has its equivalent in Oriya in the form « cāl » with long vowel and dental « l », as is also the case in Gujarati, where we have « cāl » and not « căḷ », as expected—both were derived from MIA « calla < (OIA) *calya » rather than OIA « cal ») would then be from « calyāmi > callāmi > cālaĩ, cālē »; so « karẽ, karī » from « karōmi >karami > karaĩ) » and « ambhē cālū (ambhē karũ) » would be from « asmē kurmaḥ >*karama ». Maithili and Magahi present an agreement with Bengali: in both of these Magadhan speeches we have « calī, cali » and « calũ », equally for both the numbers. Hindi singular « calũ » —plural « calẽ » are from a sg. « calāmi », and a generalized pl. affix « -ẽ », which would seem to be of pronominal origin.

But it is curious that Gujarati, on the other side of India, should present a parallel to Bengali, in having the Passive Form as the source of the First Person Plural in the Present Tense. Like OB and MB sg. « maĩ (mui) » (earlier « haũ = *ahakam ») « karõ » and pl. « amhē karīaï, kariē, karī », Gujarati has, sg. « hũ karũ », pl. « amē karīē ». From an analysis of the forms in the ŚKK, Shahidullah clearly established that it was a case in OB and MB of singular « haũ karõ », then « maĩ karõ », and plural « amhē karīaï, karīē ». We have the old situation still surviving in the Chakma dialect of Bengali in the Chittagong Hill Tracts—মুই যাঃ « mui dzāṅ » *I go* (= yāmi), pl. আমি যেই « āmi dzēi » *we go* (= *yāyatē for gamyatē); also মুই যেইআঃ « mui dzēiyāṅ » *I went*, pl. আমি যিএই « āmi dziēi » *we went*, where we have a past base without the « -il- » suffix to which the old present personal affixes are added.

941, *l.* 11: *correct to* Grammatik.

945, *after l.* 14, *add new line*: Dakhni « calyā, calā ».

948, *l.* 31, *add, before*, etc.: —Ādi-kāṇḍa (ed. Nalinī-kānta Bhaṭṭaśāli), p. 77: ধনুক টঙ্কার শুনি বিশ্বামিত্র হাসি। হেন কালে ধাইয়া আইল তাড়কা রাক্ষসী।। « dhanuka-ṭaṅkāra śuni Biśwāmitra hāsi, hēna kālē dhāïyā āïla Tāḍakā Rākṣasī » *Viswamitra laughed hearing the twang of the bow; and immediately the Ogress Tāḍakā came running;* p. 106, সন্ধান পূরিয়া রাম আকাশ পানে চাই। পলাইয়া রৈল রাক্ষস দেখিতে না পাই।। « sandhāna pūriyā Rāma ākāśa-pānē cāï: palāïyā raïla Rākṣasa, dēkhitē nā pāi » *drawing his bow to the full, Rāma looked at the sky, but the Demon lived on by running away, no one could see him*, etc.

949, *after l.* 24, *add*:

Also in the Chakma Dialect of Chittagong Hill Tracts: মুই যেইয়াং—আমি যিয়েই; তুই যিয়ছ্—তুমি যিয়; তে যিয়ে—তারা যিয়ন্ « mui dzēiyaṅ—āmi dziyēi; tui dziyas—tumi dziya; tē dziyē—tārā dziyan » *I, we, thou—you, he, they—went* (base যিয় « dziya < yāta- », without « -illa- > -il- », plus affixes from the present forms « mui dzāṅ—āmi dzēi, tui dzēis—tumi dza; tē dzāě —tārā dzān » (*see* Satish Chandra Ghosh, চাকমা জাতি 'Cākmā-jāti, or The Chakma People: Pictures of their Life, and their History,' Calcutta, 1316, Bengali Year, pp. 324–326).

956, *l.* 4: *read* câlī, jâṛī.

959, *l.* 9, *after 'petted', add, a name of Rādhā* (particularly in Vaishnava poetry).

960, *after l.* 25, *add*:

Cf. Also Early Awadhi (Tulasī-dāsa RCM, Bāla-kāṇḍa, after *dōhā* 251): « jāu̯ janateũ, binu bhaṭa bhuwi, bhāī,—tau̯ panu kari hoteũ na hāsāī » (*Janaka says*:) *if I had known, O Brothers, that in this world there are no heroes, then I would not have become a laughing-stock by taking this oath.*

961: *head-line*: *correct to* FUTURE.

966, *l.* 19: *after* Eastern Hindi, *add* (e.g. Tulasī-dāsa: « (kathā) bhāṣā-baddha karabi maĩ sōī, sō-saba hētu kahaba maĩ gāī » *that story is to be composed by me in the vernacular: for these reasons, it is to be narrated by me by singing*; « prāna-priya Siya jānibī, nija kiṅkarī kari mānibī » *Sītā is to be regarded as beloved like life, she is to be accepted as thy slave, etc.*).

968, *l.* 13: *read* is *for* in.

968, *l.* 29, *after* Construction), *add*: in addition to dialects of Vernacular Hindōstānī (cf. LSI, IX, pp. 51, 62), this Neuter Impersonal Construction is found also in Dakhani, e.g. « chokrē nē gayā » *the boy went*, literally *by-the-boy it-was-gone* (cf. LSI, IX, p. 186). We now hear in the streets of Delhi from Panjabi refugees neuter constructions with intransitive verbs, like « tum-nē kab āyā » *when did you arrive?* for « tum kab āyē, āyī »).

973, *after line* 27, *add new para*:

The employment of the Passive Past Participle (Transitive as well as Intransitive), like English dialectal *I done it, he gone home*, appears to have been established in MIA, during the transitional period (200 B.C.–A.D. 200), if not earlier. In the form of the 'Gandhārī' Prakrit as used in the Niya documents from Central Asia, this use is quite common (cf. Sukumar Sen, 'Comparative Grammar of MIA', Linguistic Society of India, Calcutta, 1951, pp. 119 ff.). This was also taken up in medieval Sanskrit writings of a popular origin: e.g. the 'Aparādha-bhañjana-stōtra' of Śankarācārya: « tvat-pādāmbhōja-yugaṃ kṣaṇam api na manasā smṛtō'haṃ kadāpi »; verse 2, « kva dhyānaṃ tē kva cârcā, kva ca manu-japanam naiva kiñcit kṛtō'ham ».

975, *ll.* 7, 8: *In place of the last sentence in these two lines, substitute:*

Cf. Bhojpuri « ham dēlī, ham rahalī » *I gave, I stayed*, etc. This « -ī- » affix appears to be taken over from the present first person: see additional note on page 935, *ll.* 11–14, *ante*.

975, *l.* 9, *from end*: *read* « pảṛilāhō̃ » *for* « pāṛilāhō̃ ».

975, *l.* 23, *after* intransitive, *add*: (with these « -ilāhō̃ » forms, the subject is not generally given, but where it is given, it is both মো « mō̃ » and আম্হে « āmhē ».

977, *l.* 18: *first word, correct as follows* (« *acchyatē », passive of « √acch », rather than « *acchāmi or acchāmaḥ »; cf. « bhūyatē, *bhavyatē »; and « *asyatē » would be the source of « hai », rather than « *asāmi, *asāmaḥ » in place of « asmi, smaḥ »).

984, *l.* 19: *correct the first* বুয়িল *to* বুইল.

990, *ll.* 15–19: Tarapada Mukherji, in a careful study of the paleography of the unique MS. of the ŚKK, has shown that the form নিবোঁক « nibōka » is wrong—the -ক « -ka » is to go with the next word (*see* BSOAS, London,

Vol. XXXI, pt. II, 1968, p. 328): the reading of the line will be « pāchē tōka nibō̃ Kabilāsē » *after this I shall take you to Kailāsa.* So this « -ka » affix is not added as a pleonastic future form of « nibō̃ ».

990, *l.* 26: *add*: It is to be noted that in the grammar of Padre Assumpçam, the « -ka » affix is used for the plural also: e.g. « tahana corileq = corilen » *they did.*

993, *last line, after* 'e.g.' *add*: MIA « aha-ka-m, tva-ka-m, OIA (Rig-Veda) asa-ka, sa-ka- (Kauṣītakī Brāhmaṇa), yāma-k-i (Śatapatha Brāhmaṇa, etc.), sa-kā, sa-ka-, ya-ka-, ya-kā, asa-ka- », etc.; and note also . . . (I am indebted to Professor Sukumar Sen for drawing my attention to these OIA forms occurring in the Vedic texts).

997, *l.* 11. Thus in Bhojpuri, we have a future affix « -lau, -lõ < laü »; in Western Rajasthani, we have « -lā » masculine, « -lī » feminine, added to the present, to indicate the future (L. P. Tessitori, 'Notes on the Grammar of Old Western Rajasthani', separate reprint, pp. 75, 76).

1000, *l.* 19: *Before* By repeating, *add*: When the subject is different from that of the finite verb in the sentence, we have a sort of absolute construction, with the participle in -ইতে « -itē » used only once: e.g. ঈশ্বর থাকিতে এরূপ পাপের শাস্তি হয় না « Īśwara thākitē, ē-rūpa pāpēra śāsti haya nā » *While God is there, there is no punishment for such sin?*; তার এমন ভাই থাক্‌তে সে কষ্ট পায় « tār èman bhāi thāktē, sē kaṣṭa pāy » *with such a brother living, he suffers*; আমি যাইতে সে আসিল « āmi jāitē, sē āsila » *on my going (lit. I going), he came.*

In expressions like তাহাকে কেহও রাগিতে দেখে নাই « tāhākē kēha-ō rāgitē dēkhē nāi » *no one saw him getting into a fit of anger*; আমি রামকে গান গাহিতে শুনিয়াছি « āmi Rāmakē gāna gāhitē śuniyāchi » *I have heard Rama singing*, etc., the construction in its origin is of the locative absolute of OIA (*bhāvē saptamī*), but it has taken up a slightly syntactical diversity.

1000, *l.* 21: *delete example* আমি যাইতে সে আসিল, etc.

1000, *ll.* 24–25: *delete example* তার এমন ভাই থাক্‌তে, *etc.*

1000, *l.* 27: *add, after* etc.: cf. Hindōstānī « mērē dēkhtē-hī-dēkhtē wŏh paidā bhī huā, jawān bhī huā, aulād-wālā bhī huā, aur marā bhī; šikār khēltē-khēltē thak gayā », etc.

1001, *l.* 1, *add, within brackets*: also D. C. Phillott 'Hindustani Stumbling-blocks', London, 1909, pp. 69, 77.

1001, *l.* 5: *after* 'we stitch', *add some other instances*: « din caṛhtē-caṛhtē = din carhnē kē waqt » *about 7 or 8 o'clock*; « dō bajtē-bajtē » *before 2 o'clock*; « din ḍubtē-ḍubtē » *before sunset*; « suntē kē sāth = suntē hī, sunnē-kē sāth » *immediately on hearing*; « mērē hōtē huē » *when I was there*; « hukm miltē hī, maĩ rawānā huā » *immediately on the order coming, I started*; « mērē hukm dētē hī wŏh calā gayā » *immediately I gave the order, he departed*, etc.

1014, § **747**. The derivation proposed here of the Bengali Infinite in -ইতে « -itē » does not appear to be tenable. It is not a new formation in Bengali, and it has to be taken in its *ensemble* with other similar or equivalent forms in the sister forms of NIA. The Infinite in -ইতে « itē » is doubtless the same as the Present Participle in « -it- < -ant- », put in the locative (as discussed in pp. 999 ff.). This « -itē » Infinitive indicates: (1) wish, e.g. আমি খাইতে চাই « āmi khāitē cāi » *I wish to eat*; (2) ability, তুমি গাহিতে পার ? « tumi gāhitē pāra ? » *can you sing ?*; (3) permission: যাইতে দাও « jāitē dāō » *let him go*; (4) prohibition: এ কাজ করিতে নাই « ē kāj karitē nāi » *this thing is not to be done*; (5) insistence or necessity: তোমায় যাইতে(ই) হইবে « tōmāy jāitē(i) haibē » *you are to (= you must) go*; (6) inception, e.g. খাইতে লাগিল « khāitē lāgila » *began to eat*; or (7) intention: খাইতে গিয়াছে « khāïtē giyāchē » *has gone to eat*; etc., আমাকে (আমায়) যাইতে হইবে « āmākē (āmāy) jāitē haibē » *I shall have to go* is literally, *for-me in-the-act-of-going it-is-to-be*, the earlier equivalents of a phrase like this would be in OIA-MIA. « *asma-kṛtē, jāantahi (= gacch-at-i, locative of the *śatṛ* form), bhavitavyam ». So সে চলিতে পারে « sē calitē pārē » *he can walk* (< *sa-kaḥ calantahi (= cal-at-i) pārayati ». Cf. Hindi « prēma-kahānī, sakhi, sunata suhāwē » = Early Bengali *প্রেম-কাহিনী সখি! শুনিতে সুহায় « prēma-kāhinī, sakhi! śunitē suhāy »; « jātē ḍartā hū̃ = jātē huē » *I feel afraid while going*; « maĩ-nē aurat-kō jagtē dēkhā » *I saw the woman awake*; « usē dauṛ kar jātē (huē) dēkhā » *he was seen while running*; « us-nē kabhī ghoṛe-kā na'l bandhtē (huē) (or bā̃dhtē) nahĩ dēkhā hai » *he has never seen a horse being shod*; etc., cf. also Early Awadhi (Tulasī-dāsa): « Lakhana kahēu, muni! sujasa tumhārā, tumhahi achata kō baranaī pārā » *Lakshman said: O Sage! you have reputation: you being here, who can describe the thing?*

1019, *l.* 9 *from the end*: *read* « āch » for the present and the past.

1019, *l.* 24 *add* present and *before* past.

1019, *last line*: *before* But, *add*: The forms in « -ta- » suggest the occurrence of the Present Participle base « -it- » only, not the locative in « -it-ē » in this Compound Verb form.

1027, *l.* 25: *after 'lies' add*, Bṛindābana-dāsa, 'Caitanya-Bhāgavata' *Amrita Bazar Patrika* edition, B.E. 1356; p. 248 মুঞি করিয়াছোঁ « muñi kariyāchō̃ » *I have done*; p. 252 ভাঙ্গিয়াছোঁ « bhāṅgiyāchō̃ » *I have broken.*

1029, *l.* 13: *read* « -(i)t- + -it- » + root « āch ».

1029: *Add at the bottom*:

The Causative Affix « -ā- » of Standard Bengali, from « -āwa- < -āpaya- », occurs in the Standard Colloquial also as « -ō- »: e.g. Standard Literary শিখায় « śikhāy » *he teaches* (*śikṣāpayati), Standard Colloquial « śikhōy, śĕkhōy ». By Vowel Harmony, this « -ō- » becomes « -u- »: e.g. আমি শিখাই « āmi sikhāi » *I teach* > শিখোই, শিখুই « śikhōi, śikhui ». So উঠাই, ওঠাই > উঠোই, উঠুই « uṭhāi, ōṭhāi; uṭhōi, uṭhui » *I lift*; সে শিখাচ্ছে: শিখোচ্ছে, শিখুচ্ছে « sē śikhācchē: śikhōcchē, śikhucchē » *he is teaching*, উঠাচ্ছে: উঠোচ্ছে, উঠুচ্ছে « uṭhācchē: uṭhōcchē, uṭhucchē » *he is causing to lift.* (Cf. in other cases also—দৌড়াই > দৌড়োই, দৌড়ই, দৌড়ুই « dauṛāi > daurōi, dauṛai, dauṛui » *I run*; পহুঁছাই > পঁৌছই, পঁৌছোই, পঁৌছুই « pahũchāi > paũchōi, paũchui » *I reach*, etc.). This « -ō- » in the *Calit-bhāṣā* (Standard Colloquial) is a remnant or vestige, in all likelihood, of the original « -w- » in the Causative; « *śikhāwaï > śikhōē̃ ». Cf. West Bengali (Birbhum)—জল খওআয়েঁ লিয়েঁ এসো « (jalȧ khawāē̃ liyē̃ ēsō) » = Standard Bengali জল খাওয়াইয়া লইয়া আইস « jalȧ khāoāiyā laiyā āisa » *bring him after making him drink water.* In Assamese, we have « -w- » in Causatives, e.g. « khowā » *to cause to eat*, « powā » *to cause to receive*, « ānōwā » *to cause to bring*, « ghusuwā » *to cause to remove*, « khuuwā » *to make one cause another to eat*, etc. Cf. Oriya « dibāra » *for giving*, « diyāibāra » *to cause to give* (= Bengali dēōāïbārȧ). Cf. also Early Maithil « rāta nalinī-dala sēja śōāubi, kata dēba malayaja-paṅkā: jalaja-dalana kata dēhē dēyāōba, tathu-hu hutāsana-śaṅkā » *at night she will be made to sleep in a bed of lotus petals, and so much sandal-paste will be given* (= *smeared on her person*): *how much of lotus petals will be made to put on her body—and still* (*on the top of that*) *there is the fear of* (*heat like*) *fire.*

1032, *l.* 10: *read* « pålānå » *for* « pālānå ».

1035, *l.* 3: *read* adjective passive participle *for* verbal noun; *and in line* 6, *take the semicolon before* so.

1035, *after l.* 7 *add*:

Periparastic Denominatives with root কর্ « kar » *to do* is exceedingly common in Bengali as well as other NIA. It is a device also found in Persian, and the idea has been adopted in Ogden's *Basic English*. It started as early as first MIA, as in Pali: « passāvaṃ karōti, kalahaṃ karōti, saññaṃ (= saṃjñāṃ) karōti », etc. Cf. OB « diḍha karia » for a synthetic form দঢ়াইয়া « daḍhāiyā » *making strong* in MB. There is also an agreement with Dravidian: e.g. Tamil « muttañ ceytan » *kiss made* = *kissed*; « pāvañ ceytan » *sinned*; Telugu « pāḍu cesenu » *waste made* = *wasted*; « vrayamu cesina » *expense having made* = *having spent*, etc.

1035, *l.* 26: *after* if not earlier, *add*: Grierson ('The √*acch* in Modern India', Garbe-Festgabe, 1927, pp. 24–32) insisted upon the « ṛ-cch- <√ṛ = acch » derivation. Sanskrit grammarians group together the verbs « iṣ, gam, yam, ṛ » (Pāṇini, VII, iii, 77–78). From « ṛ > ṛcchati » *goes* we have Pali « acchati », Prakrita « acchaï ». Semantic change of root, meaning *to go*, to *to become, to be*, is not uncommon: cf. English *the milk has gone sour*; Hindi « jānā » is often in the sense of « hōnā », and in Kashmiri we have « gatshun », past participle « gauv » = *go, become..*

R. L. Turner suggested « ā-kṣēti » *abides, dwells*, from « √kṣi », found in the Rig-Veda, as the source of « acch, āch, cha », etc., in NIA, but also of « ah, ha » and « akh, khē, akhalu » in NIA. ('Indian and Iranian Studies—presented to Sir George Abraham Grierson on his 85th birthday', in the 'Bulletin of the School of Oriental Studies', Vol. VIII, pp. 793 ff., 1936; and also « ākṣēti », No. 1031 in his 'Comparative Dictionary of the Indo-Aryan Languages', 1962). The Bihari forms, Bhojpuri « khē » *is*, « naj-khē » *is not*, « najkhe bā » *is not indeed*; Early Maithili « akhalu » *was*, etc., may be from the less common root « ā-kṣēti » as posed by Turner. Chakma « agē » *is, are*, « ēl » *was, were* are not satisfactorily explained in their isolation from other forms of Bengali.

1035, *begin new para from*: The most satisfactory derivation, etc.

1036, *after l.* 16: *add*: The Prakrit Grammarians accepted MIA « acch » as a form of « as » (Cf. « astēr acchaḥ », Vararuci, 'Prakrta-Prakassa'; *see* below).

1036, *after l.* 27, *add*: « achnā » is also found in Dakhani (LSI, IX, p. 197; also « ach-kar = hō-kar », LSI, IX, p. 209). In Lahndi (Hindki), we have still « achnā » in a slightly changed sense, that of *to come*.

1040, *l.* 14: There is a Skt. root « rah » *to remain*, but that looks like the new or back formation, connected with « rahita » *abandoned, deserted*, « rahas » *secret, isolated*, « vi-raha » *alone, separated*, etc. (See No. 10666 in Turner, 'Comparative Dictionary'.)

1040, *last line but one*: *read* altindischen.

1043, *before* § **771**, *add new section*:

(P) NEGATIVE VERB FORMS

770A. We have some Negative Verbs with না, ন « nā, na » prefixed to them. Thus নাহয়, নহয়, নয় « nā-hay > na-hay > nay » *it is not:* colloquially না অহই > নাহী, নাহি > নাই, নেই, নি, নে « nā-ahai > nāhī, nāhi > nāi, nēi, ni; ne » *does not exist, is not, not*; cf. গাছের উপরে ওটা মানুষ নয়, বাঁদর « gāchērȧ uparē ō-ṭā mānuṣȧ nay, bā̃darȧ » *up on the tree it is not a man, (but) a monkey*; দেশে আর মানুষ নাই (নেই), সব পশু « dēśē ārȧ mānuṣȧ nāi (nēi), sabȧ paśu » *there is no longer a man in the land, all are beasts.* But আমি বলি নাই « āmi bali nāi », colloquially আমি বলি নি « āmi bali ni » *I did not say*, with a past sense: সে বলে নাই, বলে নি « sē balē nāi, bale ni » *he did not say*: here the past sense, brought in by নাহি > নাই, নি « nāhi > nāi, ni » may be the result of the original form নাহি being from OIA « nāsīt (na+āsīt) » *did not exist.* Cf. আমি বলি না > বলিনে by Vowel Harmony « āmi bali nā > bali nē » *I do not say*; সে বলে না « sē balē nā » (never « balē nē ») *he does not say* (but by Vowel Harmony, in the first person, আমি বলি না > নে « āmi bali nā > balinē »).

We have also MB and dialectal NB √নার « nār » also লার্ « lär » < « nā-pār » *not to be able* (Assamese « no-wār »).

In MB there was a negative form নাছ « nāch » *not to be* (« na + āch »).

1043, § **771.** *Above this, add new heading.*

[Q] SOME IRREGULAR FORMS

1045, *l.* 4: *Correct to* Standard Spoken Bengali, but it occurs in East Bengali dialects, e.g. লয্যা « layyā » = লইয়া « laiyā » *having taken* = *Standard Colloquial* নিয়ে « niye ».

1047, *in Heading, below l.* 13: *correct* [P] *to* [R].

1047, *after l.* 30, *add*: Instances from Pali have been given by Ramaprasad Chaudhuri, M.A., in the VSPdP, বাংলা ভাষায় পালি শব্দ ও ইডিয়ম, Vol. 59, 1953, pp. 54 ff.: « thutiṃ katvā katvā kathēsi; ahaṃ taṃ pucchantō pucchantō; saṃkhipitvā saṃkhipitvā; gacchantē gacchantē kālē; tumhē gahapatikena dinnaṃ bhuñjitvā bhuñjitvā supatha (= *sleep*); ābhā chijjitvā chijjitvā patanti viya; rathō tālavanaṃ chijjitvā chijjitvā; āsajja āsajja avacāsi; upaneyya upaneyya avōca », etc.

1049, *l.* 4, *add:* জেদাজেদি « jēdājēdi » *by mutual importunacy or pressure* (< Perso-Arabic zidd < Arabic ḍidd).

1049, *Heading in the middle of page*: *correct* [Q] *to* [S].

1050, *after l.* 18 *add.* The Altaic and Sino-Tibetan (Tibeto-Burman) languages also have the same device of Compound Verbs. Thus, in Central Asian Turki of East Turkistan (Sin-Kiang), as given in Robert Berkley Shaw's 'Sketch of the Turki Language', Calcutta, 1878, p. 78: « sàt-ip àl-màq » *take away by purchase* < *having sold, to take*: cf. Bengali কিনিয়া লওয়া « kiniyā laoā »; « àl-ip bàr-màq » *having taken, to go* = *take away*: cf. Bengali লইয়া যাওয়া « laiyā jāoā »; « yet-ip gàl-màq » *having reached a limit, to remain over* = *to exceed*; « küyüb bir-maq » *having burnt, to give* = *to burn, to give over to burning*, cf. Bengali পুড়াইয়া দেওয়া « puṛāïyā dēoā ». So Burmese « ta pit » = মারিয়া ফেলা « māriyā phēlā », « ca twa » = পড়িয়া যাওয়া « paṛiyā jāōā », « ne twa » = ভুলিয়া যাওয়া « bhuliyā jāoā », « pe hta » = দিয়া রাখা « diyā rākhā », « pei hta » = ভেজাইয়া রাখা « bhejāïyā rākhā », etc.

1050, *after l.* 25. This idiom is found in MIA (Pali): e.g. examples quoted by Ramaprasad Chaudhuri in the VSPdP article mentioned above (under p. 1047, l. 30): « patitvā gataṃ » = পড়িয়া গেল « paṛiyā gela »; « āliṅgitvā ādāya = আলিঙ্গিয়া লইয়া « āliṅgiyā laiyā »; « maccū ādāya gacchati » = মৃত্যু লইয়া যায় « mṛtyu laiyā jāy »; « yāguṃ pacitvā adāsi » = জাউ

পাকাইয়া বা রাধিঁয়া দিল « jāu pākāiyā (rā̃dhiyā) dila », « sampādetvā adaṃsu » = করিয়া দিল « kariyā dila »; « likhitvā ṭhapati » = লিখিয়া রাখে « likhiyā rākhe »; « āgantuṃ na dassanti » = আসিতে দিবে না « āsitē dibē nā »; « idān' assa dhammaṃ sotuṃ labhissāmi » = এখন তাহার ধর্মকথা শুনিতে পাইব « ekhan tāhārȧ dharma-kathā śunitē pāiba »; etc.

1056, *at the end, add*:

1053–1056: APPENDIX. *Add, at the end, on page* 1056:

§ **781**. Below are given two lines from a poem by Rabindranath Tagore, which are worked back successively, word for word, into the preceding stages, from New or Modern Bengali of the twentieth century A.D. to Spoken Vedic of *c.* tenth century B.C., seeking to show the development of Indo-Aryan through 30 centuries, from Old Indo-Aryan to the current phase of New Indo-Aryan. The lines are from one of Tagore's most famous mystic-spiritual poems, the সোনার তরী « Sonārȧ Tarī » or *the Golden Boat*, and run as follows:

গান গেয়ে তরী বেয়ে কে আসে পারে।
দেখে যেন মনে হয়—চিনি উহারে।।

« gānȧ gēyē tårī bēyē kē āsē pārē:
dēkhē jēnå månē håy—cini uhārē »

[gɑn geĕe tori beĕe ke ɑʃe pɑre,
dekhe ʤæno mone ɦɔĕ, ʧini ufiɑre]

Singing a song, rowing (her) boat, who is it that comes across?
Looking (at her) it seems in my mind, I know her.

These two lines are in good modern Bengali, but there are two words which require a comment. The word তরী « tarī » *boat* is not current in colloquial speech, it is more or less a learned Sanskrit loan in literary Bengali, although it will be universally understood. The more common word in colloquial Bengali would be নৌকা or নৌকো « naukā, naukō [nouko] », and a still more popular word (though now a folk or village word) would be না « nā » (or নাও « nāo », now current chiefly in East Bengal). Then the form উহারে « uhārē » is a literary and poetical archaism—the corresponding colloquial form in current Bengali would be ওরে « ōrē » (or, preferably, in the Standard Colloquial, ওকে « ōkē »).

Substituting these two words in the lines as written by the poet himself, we shall have the purely colloquial version for the present year (1970) as—

1. গান গেয়ে, না বেয়ে, কে আসে (= আশে) পারে—
দেখে যেন (= জ্যানো) মনে হয়, চিনি ওকে (or ওরে) ॥

gānȧ geye, nā beye, kē āsē pārē—
dēkhē jēnȧ manē hay, cini ōkē (ōrē).

[gan geĕe, na: beĕe, ke aʃe pare—
dekhe ɟʒæno mone ɦɔĕ, c͡ʃini oke (ore)]

2. In Middle Bengali of *c.* A.D. 1500, this was something like—
গান গায়্যা (গাইহ্যা), নাও বায়্যা (বাইহ্যা), কে আশ্যে (আইশে) পারে।
দেখ্যা (দেইখ্যা) জেন্অ (জেন্হ, জেহেন) মনে হোএ, চিনী (চিনহীয়ে) ওআরে
(ওহারে ; ওহাকে) ॥

In phonetic transcription—

[ga :n gajjɛ (gaiɦea), nao bajjɛ (baiɦea), ke aiʃɛ pare—
dekhɛ (deikhea) ɟʒenɦɔ (ɟʒeɦenɔ) mɔnɛ ɦoɛ, cʃini: (cʃinɦiĕ) o(ɦ)are
(oɦake)]

3. In Old Bengali (Old Gauḍa Speech) of *c.* A.D. 1100—
গাণ গাহিআ, নাৱ বাহিআ, কে আইশই (আৱিশই) পারহি (পালহি)।
দেখিআ জৈহণ মণে (মণহি) হোই—চিন্হিঅই ওহারহি (ওহাকহি) ॥

[ga:ṇɔ̇ gaɦia, na:wɔ baɦia, ke aïʃɔï (awiʃɔi) pa:rɔɦi (pa :lɔɦi),
dekhia ɟʒɔiɦɔṇɔ mɔṇe (mɔṇɔɦi) ɦo:i—c͡ʃiṇɦiɔï oɦarɔɦi (oɦakɔhi)]

4. In Māgadhī Apabhraṃśa of *c.* A.D. 700—
গাণঁ গাহিঅ, নাৱঁ বাহিঅ, কই (কি) আৱিশই পারহি (পালহি)।
দেক্খিঅ জইহণঁ (জইশণঁ) মণহি হোই—চিণ্হিঅই ওহঅলহি (ওহঅরহি :
ওহকহি) ॥

[ga:ṇã ga:ɦia, na:wã ba:ɦia, kaï (ki) a:wiʃaï pa:raɦi (pa:laɦi)—
dekkhia ɟʒaïɦaṇã (ɟʒaïʃaṇa) maṇaɦi ɦo:i, c͡ʃiṇɦiaï oɦaaraɦi (oɦaalaɦi,
oɦakaɦi)]

5. Māgadhī Prakrit, *c.* A.D. 200—

গাণং গাধিআ (গাধিত্তা), নাৱং বাহিঅ (বাধিত্তা), কগে (কএ, কে) আৱিশদি পারধি (পালধি)।

দেক্কিঅ (দেক্খিত্তা) যাদিশণ° মণধি ভোদি (হোদি), চিণহিঅদি অমুশ্শকলধি (অমুশ্শকদে)

[gɑ:ṇaã gɑ:dɦia (gɑ:dɦitta:), nɑ:waã bɑ:ɦia (wɑ:hitta:), kaγe (kage, ke:) ɑ:wiʃaδi pɑ:laδi: —

dekkhia (dekkhittɑ:) ɟɑ:δiʃaṇa manaδhi bɦo:δı (ɦo:δi), cʃiṇhiaδi ɑmuʃʃakalaδhi (amuʃʃakaδe:)]

6. Prācya or Eastern Prakrit of *c.* 500 B.C.—

গানং গাথেত্বা নাৱং ৱাহেত্বা ককে (কে) আৱিশতি পালধি (পালে)।

দেক্খিত্বা যাদিশনং (যাদিশং) মনধি (মনশিঁ) হোতি (ভোতি), চিন্হিয়তি অমুশ্শ কলাধি (কলে, কতে)।

[gɑ:naã gɑ:the:twɑ: nɑ:waã wɑ:ɦe:twɑ: , kake: (ke:) ɑ:wiʃati pɑ:laδɦi (pɑ:le:),

dekkhitwɑ: jɑ:diʃaã mɑnɑdɦi (mɑnɑsi) ɦo:ti (bho:ti), cinɦiyati amuʃʃa-kaladɦi (-kale:, kate:)]

7. Spoken or Dialectal Vedic, *c.* 1000 B.C.—

গানং গাথযিত্বা, নাৱং ৱাহয়িত্বা, ককঃ (= কঃ) আৱিশতি পারধি (পারে)।

দৃক্ষিত্বা (= দৃষ্ট্বা) যাদৃশং মনোধি (মনসি) ভৱতি—চিহ্ন্যতে অমুষ্য (+করধি, করে, কৃতে)॥

[gɑ:naŋ gɑ:thajit:wɑ: , nɑ:waã wɑɦajitwɑ: , kakah (= kah) ɑ:wiʃati pɑ:radɦi (pɑ:re:),

dr̥kʃitwɑ: (= dr̥ʃṭwɑ:) jɑ:dr̥çam mɑno:dɦi (mɑnɑsi) bɦɑwati, ciɦnjate: ɑmuʃja (+karadɦi, kare:, kr̥te:)]

* * * *

There has thus taken place a continuous development of the Primitive Indo-European Speech through the Aryan or Indo-Iranian and then through the Indo-Aryan as in Vedic times down to the present age of New Indo-Aryan. The stream has maintained its identity, although it has been profoundly modified in its course, and has been influenced in all directions by newer freshets and waters from other sources.

An attempt has been made to trace this history as a continuous development in the preceding pages. But there are very many obscurities, and vast *lacunae*, which we can only hope will be filled up by subsequent research, with newer materials as yet unsalvaged, and newer and more effective methods (with the help of instruments) which the progress of linguistics as a human science is ever discovering for us and putting them to use.

* * * *

We can only close with words of benediction from some of the ancient grammarians of India:

« Śaṃ Śabdaiḥ »

With Words, Welfare.

« Sarvajñaṃ tad ahaṃ vandē, parañ jyōtis tamōpaham,
pravṛttā yan-mukhād Dēvī sarva-bhāṣā-sarasvatī »

I adore that all-knowing Supreme Light, dispelling darkness,
From whose mouth has issued the Goddess, the sacred stream of all Speech.

And with the Prayers from the Rig-Veda:

« cōdayitrī sunṛtānāṃ, cētantī sumatīnām : yajñaṃ dadhē Sarasvatī »

Inspirer of all pleasant things, rouser of all good thoughts, Sarasvatī, Speech, accept our adoration!

« mahō arṇah Sarasvatī pra cētayati kētunā: dhiyō viśvā vi rājati »

Sarasvati or Speech, the Mighty Flood: she rouses up with her light, and brightens all intellects.

and,

« aham rāṣṭrī, saṅgamanī vasūnām, cikituṣī, prathamā yajñiyānām »

I, Speech, am of the State: I gather for men all wealth; I am the Wise, the Thinking One; I am the First of the Adorable Ones.

EPILOGUE

The *Origin and Development of the Bengali Language* was prepared in its first draft in London in 1920–1921 under the supervision of Dr. Lionel D. Barnett of the Department of Oriental Books and Manuscripts in the British Museum Library, and Professor of Sanskrit and Indian Archaeology at the University of London. I was a student of the *School of Oriental Studies* (later *Oriental and African Studies*) in the University as a Government of India State Scholar in Sanskrit (in its Linguistic or Philological side), and Dr. Barnett was my officially appointed guide, teacher and supervisor. He watched over my studies, and helped me with advice; and when I was preparing the first draft of my work I read every page of it with him, and this was virtually the first edition of the work. Then I wrote out my work in my own hand, from which four lithograph copies were made, and three of these were submitted to the University of London for its D.Litt. degree. This formed a sort of second edition of the work. My examiners recommended it for the award of the degree, which was conferred upon me by the University of London on 20th July 1921.

Subsequently after that, Sir George Abraham Grierson read through the manuscript and wrote down his comments and criticisms to help in publishing it, and so did also Professor Jules Bloch in Paris. I feel very grateful to them for the kind care which they showed in helping me to make my work more presentable. With their notes, after coming back to Calcutta in November 1922, when my book was accepted by my University for publication, I prepared the press-copy in my own hand once more, and this press-copy formed a sort of a third edition of my work, in manuscript, and it was this third edition, so to say, which was finally published from the Calcutta University Press, in 1926, with all the proofs being seen by me. In this way Professor Jules Bloch's observation that a serious scientific work, in the humanities particularly, should be printed and published for the first time in its third edition, came to be true for the *Origin and Development of the Bengali Language*.

Only 500 copies of the book were printed, and these were sold out within a few years. The book then remained out of print for over four decades. The demand for the book went on increasing with the years, not only in Bengal but throughout the rest of India as well, and also abroad. I received frequent requests for bringing out a second edition, requests which were often pressing and urgent. But numbers of still more urgent and immediate pre-occupations, both scholarly and otherwise, gave me no time to attack this rather long work for a second edition. I used, however, regularly to note down in my personal copy the things I thought should be rectified or newly added.

In the meanwhile, some Japanese students of Indian linguistics brought out from Tokyo a photographic reproduction of the book in 1961 for their own study and use, and the University Microfilm Co. of Ann Arbor, Michigan, brought out an offset reprint of the first edition, and this met the demand partially. Pressing offers came from many publishers, but I could seriously take it up only during last year, 43 years after my book was out. It was felt that a fully revised new edition would take a long time to print *de novo*, and I was reaching my eightieth year. Finally, it was decided to bring an offset reprint from the original edition, with a third volume for the *Additions and Corrections* and the *Index of Bengali Words*, completely re-written and printed afresh, as the basis for an offset printing, to go with the reprint of the main work in two volumes, in the same style. This has finally been done, after a good deal of labour: and in this way, the Second Printed Edition of *the Origin and Development of the Bengali Language* has been placed before the public this year, 1971, with a Supplementary Volume, nearly half a century (45 years) after the appearance of the First Edition in 1926 in two volumes.

I have nothing more to add by way of an *Epilogue* or *Envoi* to this new edition of my book, which has been constantly with me for over 50 years, and I am thankful that the work has been of some help to others both at home and abroad. Through the march of Time during these years, Nature and Man have both changed enormously—Nature by being brought under the control of man for his material purposes, and Man by successfully seeking to attain a new kind of transformation which is bringing to him the status almost of a Divinity who is the master of creation. But he has not been able to remove the menace of over-population which threatens to lead to his ultimate destruction, and he is losing more and more his power to know himself and to guide himself in the attainment of inner knowledge, peace and harmony, and happiness. The never-ending process of Becoming is there, and there seems to be a Purpose, not understood by us, in this continually changing Destiny of Man. The bounds of man's knowledge and information (if not always of understanding) are extending in a geometrical progression; and newer and newer and at the same time more and more complicated methods of scientific investigation are extending the horizon of the different sciences—the old ones, and the many new ones which are coming into existence. Scientific Linguistics, a science which is some 3,000 years old in India, and which started its career as a new science and discipline in Europe only about two centuries ago, is also within the line of this progress. During the last two generations that the book has been in use, some new and very great developments have shown themselves in Linguistics. The gradual emergence of *Synchronistic Linguistics* (*Descriptive and Structural*, as it has also been called) is a very notable thing in this connexion. If we take it as a legitimate case of evolution in the science, it would be the most natural thing. The old, if it is scientifically conceived in its basis, finds its fulfilment in the new. « Śraddhāvān labhatē jñānam »—*those who have reverence attain to knowledge*, and the evolution of new ideas and methods, with new and unforeseen aids from scientific instruments and gadgets, does not entirely put out of court the old methods, especially when the Old is always ready to accept and adopt what the New has to offer, viz. viewpoints and methods which are sure and certain, and are of permanent value, and are not just of an experimental nature.

But sometimes our enthusiasm for the New makes us forget the value and the services of the Old, and our eagerness in an impassioned quest for the New has sometimes made some of its younger advocates consider the achievements of the Past through the old methods, when the new methods were in the process of evolution, as useless junk which is to be dismissed with impatience. The Old, however, still continues to prove to be helpful: *eppur si muove*, 'still it moves'—so it can be said of the old *Diachronistic* (or *Historical and Comparative*) *Method*, which is now sought to be relegated to the limbo of oblivion by some of the more ardent advocates of the modernistic Synchronistic Method. Unfortunately there is no general agreement among the masters and protagonists of the new method, particularly in the matter of a set of sane and precise and universally accepted technical terms (in the same language of science, like English, for instance), replacing as well as enlarging the current ones, as being very vital and necessary tools for research. Each single master in the new line seems to be ploughing his solitary furrow. And often it is like *beaucoup de bruit, très peu de résultat*, when we consider these new terms and the new explanations and 'discoveries' which these terms seek to indicate. While the Synchronistic Method is progressing, there are steadily growing objections to its ideas, methods and findings, and to its 'inadequacies', and the need for rethinking is being pressed by competent critics of the New. Some trenchant criticisms are also appearing. The old Indian poet said, « purāṇam ity ēva na sādhu sarvam », *all that is* old *is not good or correct*; but it is equally true also that « navīnam ity api na sādhu sarvam », *all that is* new *also is not good.*

I need not enter into this war of methods and ideologies, or controversy, or discussion, or dialogue. It has to be resolved by a harmonious combination of the Old and New, as it was suggested in a not very competent attempt on my part (as published in 1962 in my paper on 'The Levels of Linguistic Analysis' in the Proceedings of the Ninth International Congress of Linguists held at Harvard University and the Massachusetts Institute of Technology in the U.S.A., Mouton & Co., the Hague, Holland, 1964, pp. 283–293), and in a series of papers by eminent linguisticians at the Tenth International Congress of Linguists held at Bucharest, Rumania, in August-September, 1967.

I bring all this in, as some of the advocates of the new method might question the propriety of bringing out a new offset edition of a 45-year-old book following the Diachronistic Comparative and Historical Method (but open nevertheless to all new ideas and methods that are valid) at this late hour.

To the firm of Messrs George Allen and Unwin Ltd. in London go my thanks for offering to take up the work for this new edition, and I am very happy that finally it has been printed with characteristic efficiency and beauty under their care.

I take this occasion to express my grateful thanks to my pupils and friends, who helped me in many ways, particularly to my Secretary Sri Sisir Kumar Banerji B.A., and my Research Assistant Sri Anil Kumar Kanjilal M.A., for their most devoted and efficient help for all these years.

Apart from some other work in the various related fields in the Human Sciences, like Linguistics, History, Culture, Literature, Travelogues, etc., this Second Edition of the *Origin and Development of the Bengali Language* marks the *finale* of a long career devoted to study and research and guidance of younger workers covering more than sixty years and extending over the whole of India. On my 81st birthday, *26 November 1970*, I can only say, when I am nearing the close of my career, during which I have received all through and from all quarters only good and no evil that I can think of, only sympathy and affection and helpfulness, I wish the best of success to all junior workers in the subject, with joy and happiness in their work. I can also say, in all humility and in all thankfulness—

« nunc dimittis servum tuum, Domine, in pace »:

and

« prajñānânanda-rūpāya priyāya ca rasâtmanē,
samarpyatē karma-phalaṃ Tasmāi viśva-vidē satē || »

'SUDHARMĀ'
16 Hindusthan Park
Calcutta 29
(*19 September 1971 : Mahālayā Day*)

SUNITI KUMAR CHATTERJI

INDEX OF BENGALI WORDS

[The Numbers refer to Pages in the Supplementary Volume]

অন্ত—55
অঙ্গাঙ্গীভাবে—57
অছেল—55
অজু—55
অজুহাৎ—84
অজেদ—55
অড—55
অনিমিথ, অনিমেথ—62
-অনিয়া,-অ'নে,-উনে,-ওনে—72
অপ‍্চ—53
অবলা—50
অজ্ঞ—88
অভিধান-জাত—80
অযুত—89
অলী—55
অশথ—50

আইট—77
আইনতঃ—80
আইহত—64
আউট—50
আউট-কুড়া—50
আওঁয়ানি—74
আইঠা—63
আইঠুয়া—63
আউঠা—63
আঁকড়া—78
আচ—62
-আচ—77
আটকুড়ো—50
আঁধুয়া—59
আঁথেজ—70
আগনি—50

আগাড়ী—78
আগুন, আগুনি—50
আগুয়ান—73
-আচি—77
আচাভুআ—57, 62, 65
আট—77
আটাসে'—58, 66
আডিড—59
আড্চিা—59
আদরা—37
আধেলা—76
আধ‍্লা—76
-আনিয়া, -আনে—73
আন‍্কা, আন‍্কো—76
আন্থা, আন্থো—76
আঙ্কুয়া—59
আপনি, আপনে—83
আপিস-হায়—84
আবোলা—50
আমরুল—79
আমলা-হায়—84
আমানী—74
আমারী—69
আমি—83
আমিনি,-নী—74
আমুহি—83
আমহে—83
আয়লা-সয়লা—70
আয়ত্ত—64
আলজিভ—50
আলাল—74
আশগন্দ—67
আশথ—50

আশ-শাওড়া, আশ-শেওড়া—67
আষ্টি—89
আষ্টেক—77
(আ)সওয়ার—40
আস্ত—53
আস্তা—53
আহা—68
আন্ধি, আন্ধে—83

ঈদ—49, 57
ঈদকুড়ি, ঈদ্‌কুড়ি—57
ঈদারা,-ঈদেরা—57, 82
ঈদাস—57
ইড‍্লৌ—40
-ইতা—75
-ইতে—98, 99
ইন্দাস—57
-ইয়ান,-এন—75
-ইয়ানিয়া,-আনে—75
ইস্কুপ‍্—42

উকিলান—84
উতরোল—79
-উত্তর—80
-উনে—72
উপারের-টা—78
উপ‍্মা—41
উভরোল—79
উরত, উরাত—64
উরাথ—64
উরুত, উরোত—64
উহা—91
উহারে—104

এইডা—88
এইতা—88
এইতান—88
এওৎ—64
একছড়া—88
একলাই—70
একানে—73
একুন—54
এজ, কেল—58
এটা—78
এতটুকু(ন)—88
এত্তটুকু(ন)—88
এথেকে—67
-এন—75
এনারা—84
এ-বেলা—52
এব্‌লা—52
এঁটো—63
এঁঠো—63

ওআন—84
ওকে—104
ওক্ত—55
ওটা—78
ওনারা—84
-ওনে—72
ও-বেলা—52
ওব্‌লা—52
ওয়াড়—55
ওরে—104
ওহাড়—55
ওহান—84
ওহাঁ—91

কই—91
কইছে—60
ক'চ্ছে—60
কড়কা—62
কড়থা—62
কত—77
কতক, কতেক—77
কমাও—72
করজ, করজা—70
করধা—70
করম্‌চা—52
করিছে—60
ক'র্‌ছে—60
কলাছড়া—88
কলিকাতাস্থ—81
কহিছে—60
কাগজাৎ—84
কাছের-টি—78
কাঞ্জিলাল—75
কাঠ-শিঙ্গেল—75
কাঠুরে—78
কাতি,-তী—76
কাতিয়ান—76
কাত্যেন—76
কান্‌-কুআ, কান্‌-কুও—54
কান্‌কো—54, 76
কান্দনিয়া—72
কান্দানিয়া—73
কামাই—72
কাল—53
কাল-কচু—53
কাল-কাশুন্দা—53
কালকূট—53
কাল-নাগিনী—53
কাল-পেঁচা—53
কাল-সাপ—53
কালা—53
কালো—53
কাল্‌—53
কাস্তে—78
কাহন—68
কি—41
কি করিয়া—86
কুও—54
কুঠিহায়—84
কুমারপাড়া—37
কুয়া—54
কুহাসা—79
কূআ—54
কৃশ্চান—56
কেউঁরে—79
কেঙ্‌রে—79
কেরাঞ্চি—77
কেল—58
কৈতর—37
কো—54
কোণ—40
কোয়া—55
কোয়াসা—79
কোহাসা—79
কাঁকরোল—79
কাঁচা, কাঁচকলা—54
কাঁদানে'—73
কাঁদুনে'—72
কাঁদ্‌লে-ট'াদ্‌লে—34
কুঁচি—62
কেঁদরা—40
কোঁস্তা—78
ক্যাঁদরা—40
ক্যাঁদরায় শনি—40
ক্রিশ্চান—56
ক্রেস্তাওঁ—56
ক্ষণেক—77

খড়ম—66
খড়ী—61
খতিয়ান—76
খাইছে—60
খাওয়ান-দাওয়ান—73
খাচ্ছে—60
খাজা—50
খাড়ী—36
খাতা-জাত—80
খাসী—69
খিদির—70
খিদিরপুর—70

থেদানে'—73
থেষ্টান—56
খুঁজ—92
খোঁপা—61
খি্স্তান—56
খ্রীষ্টান—56
খে্স্তান—56

গইলে—58
গঙ্গাটিকুড়ি—35
গঙ্গাস্নান—57
গজা—70
গড়িয়ান—76
গ'ড়েন—76
গম—67
গয়না—55, 59
গয়লা—55
গলাইয়া—58
গলিয়ে—58
গহনা—59
গাইছে—60
গাচ্ছে—60
গাছাল—75
গাত্রি—39
গাভুর—54
গাহিছে—60
গুট্ঠাকুর—52
গুণ্ডা—40, 70
গুমট, গুমোট—77
গুরু-ঠাকুর—52
গুর্ঠাকুর—52
গুল্তন, গুল্তান—69
গুহিল—55
গেরোন—56
গের্হোন—56
গো—55
গোগাঁ—37
গোড়াইত—72
গোড়াৎ—72
গোধা—49
গোবাড়িয়ান—73
গোবেড়েন—73
গোম্নে—66
গোয়ালা—55
গোরা—49
গোরো—49
গোল—69
গোসাপ—49, 55
গৌণতঃ—80
গাঁজিয়াল – 75
গাঁদা—51
গাঁদাল—74
গাঁধাল—74
গুঁই—66
গেঁজেল—75
গেঁটি—58
গেঁদা—51
গোঁআর—66
গোঁড়া—40, 70
গ্যাঁদা—51
গ্যাঁন—59

ঘটা—49
ঘটীটা—52
ঘট্টে—52
ঘড়—49
ঘর—84
ঘরো—84
ঘামাচী—77
ঘুইরে—58
ঘুম-ভাঙ্গানিয়া—73
ঘুরাইয়া—58
ঘুরিয়ে—58
ঘেরাও—72
ঘোড়—54
ঘোড়-দৌড়—54
ঘোড়া—54
ঘোড়াঞ্চি—77
ঘোল-মউনী—73
ঘোষাল—75
-চ,-আঁচ—77
চইট—77
চ'ট—77
চলিছে—60
চলিয়া—33
চলুঁৎ—93
চ'ল্ছে—60
চাইছে—60
চাউল—65
চাচ্ছে—60
চাজ—81
চাপড়া—78
চাপান—73
চাম-শিঙ্গেল—75
চাস্তলী—57
চার্জ্য—81
চার্য্য—81
চালিতা—75
চা'ল্তা, চা'ল্তে—75
চাহিছে—60
চাহিয়া—86
-চি,-আচি—77
চিতান, চিতেন—73
চিরাতা, চিরেতা—64
চেয়ে—86
চোরাই—72
চৌতিশা—72
চৌথ—40
চৌধুরী—53
চুঁচুড়া—20

ছড়—88
ছড়া—88
ছড়ি—88
ছাইতান—64
ছাতিম—64
ছাতিয়ান—64
ছাতীঅণ—64
ছাত্যান—64
ছানা-পোনা—71

ছিক-চা—70
ছিটান, ছিটেন—73
ছিষ্টি—62
ছেরানি—74
ছাঁদা—51
ছিঁচ্কা, ছিঁচ্কে—70
ছেঁদা—51
ছোঁয়াচ—77

জনি—91
জন্নু—91
জমকাল—74
জলত—86
জাইছে (যাইছে)—60
জাত—49, 64, 80
জাত-গান—49
জাতঃপাত—60
জাতিপাত—60
জামরুল—79
জাহ্নবী—72
জারুল—79
জিন—91
জুও—54
জুলি—36
জূআ—54
জেদাজেদি—103
জেদ্দাও—52
জেয়াদা—55
জো—54
জোগানে'—73
জোঙ্গড়া—63
জোল—36
জোংড়া—63
জেঁয়াচ—77
জ্ঞানতঃ—80
জ্যাদা—55
জ্যায়দা—55

ঝক্কি—63
ঝকথি—63

ঝড়—63
ঝাড়—63, 72
ঝাড়াই—72
ঝামরু—79
ঝামেলা—76
ঝুটা—63
ঝুপসা—79
ঝাঁঝাল—74
ঝুঁঝা—63

-টা—78
টাউক্যা—40
টাকুয়া—40
টাঙ্গন—40
টাট্টু—63
-টি,-টী—78
টিকর—35
টিকুরি—35
টিমি—63
:টেকো—40
টেমি—63
টেঁস—42
টাঁস—42

ঠাকুরাল—74
ঠাকুরালি—74, 75
ঠিয়েটার—71

ডান্গুলি—61
ডাণ্ডাগুলি—61
ডানা—51
ডাংগুলি—61
ডুঙ্গরী—35
ডেগ—64
ডেনা—51
ডোমাই—72
ডেঁপ—63
ডেঁপুয়া—63
ডেঁপো—63
ডেঁপো ছোকরা—63
ডেঁপোম,-মি—74
ড্যানা—51

ঢাকরিয়া, ঢাকুরিয়া—78
ঢাকুরে—78
ঢীঠ—51

ত—54
-ত—57, 80, 86
তক্লী—40
তগ্ড়া—70
তত—77
ততেক—77
তল্তা—75
তল্দা—75
-তঃ—80
তাগা—62
তাগ্ড়া—70
তাত—64
তানারা—84
তা(হা)দেব—91
তাহান—84
তা(হা)রা—91
তিনেক—77
তিরোল—79
তীশ—89
তীস—89
তু—90
তুই—90
তুই-তো-কারী—90
-তে—57
তো—54
-তো—80
তোলো—71
তাঁ—91
-ত্তর—80
-ত্র—80

থোয়েঁা—94

দড়াইয়া—101
দৎ—55
দখল—53
দরওয়াজা—55
দরজা, দরোজা—55
দলিলাৎ—84
দশেক—77
দাগা—92
দিন-ভর—51
দিনেক—77
দীপ-গাছা—47
দুআ—54
দুইছে—60
দুও—54
দুখ-দিউনে'—72
দুখ-দিয়নিয়া—72
দুচ্চার—60
দুচ্ছে—60
দুত্তিন—60
দুলাল—74
দুহা—54
দুহিছে—60
দেখ্‌বে-টেখ্‌বে—34
দেবত্র—80
দেবো'খন—91
দেবোত্তর—80
দেবোয়্যানে—91
দেয়ালা—55
দেরখো—51, 76
দেশময়—80
দেশস্থ—81
দেহালা—55
দো—54
দোয়াৎ—55
দোলাই—70, 72
দাঁইড়ে—58
দাঁড়-কাক—82
দাঁড়াইয়া—58
দাঁড়িয়ে—58
দেঁইড়ে—58

ধ'চ্ছে—60
ধরিছে—60
ধ'র্‌ছে—60
ধর্মতঃ—80
ধামাত—64
ধারানি—74
ধীরে-সুস্থে—70
ধুইছে—60
ধুচ্ছে—60
ধুমসা, ধুমসী—79
ধুমা, ধুমো—79
ধোয়—54
ধোসা—41
ধ্বস—92

ন—102
নজর—70
নয় (negative verb)—102
নর—82
নর-হাতী—82
নলিয়ান—76
ন'লেন—76
ন-হয় (negative verb)—102
না—102
না (নাও)—104
নাই (negative verb)—102
নাইঅর—51
নাইহর—51
নাও—104
নাগরালি,-লী—75
নাছ—103
না-দান—82
নাদানিয়া—82
নাদান্তে—82
না পার্য্যমানে—81
নামাল—74
নায়ের—51
নার্‌ (root)—102
নালিতা—75
না'ল্‌তে—75

না-হয় (negative verb)—102
নাহি, নাহী (negative verb)—102
নি (negative particle)—102
নিকাহিতা—81
নিছনি, নিছানি—63
নিছা—62
নিজ্জস—81
নিদ্দম—81
নির্বোক—97
নিমিতা—64
নিমকী—70
নিম্‌তা, নিম্‌তে—64
নিয়ে—103
নিযুত—89
নির্জস—70, 81
নির্জোস—70
নির্ঝঞ্ঝাট—81
নির্দম—81
নির্যস—70
নিশি-ভোর—51
নীচের-টা—78
নে (negative particle)—102
নেই (negative verb)—102
নেউছা—62
নেদানে—82
নেমন্তন্ন—67
নৈদ—67
নোড়—64, 67
নৌকা, নৌকো—104
ন্যাদানে—82
ন্যায়তঃ—80

পইট—77
পই-পই (ক'রে) বলা—49
পকেট-জাত—80
পগার—51
প'ট—77
পড়শি, পড়িশি—52
পড়িয়া—33
পড়িয়ান—76

পড়িহাএ—64
পড়িহায়—64
পড়িহাহে—64
প'ড়েন—76
পরতেথ—59
পরাণে—73
পর্মায়ু—56
প'ল—53
পলাশন—72
প'লো—53
পাইছে—60
পাইলে—58
পাখুড়ী—57
পাচ্ছে—60
পাছুয়ান—73
পাত—81
পাত-মৌড়—82
পাতলা—82
পাতি—81
পাতি-কাক—82
পাতি-কুয়া—81
পাতিনেড়ে—82
পাতি-ভাঁড়—82
পাত-মৌড়—82
পাতিল—39
পাতি-লেবু—82
পাতি-শেয়াল—82
পাতি-হাঁস—82
পাত্কুও—81
পাত্কো—81
পানীয়—49
পায়রা—55
পারুল—79
পারোঁ—94
পালাইয়া—58
পালিয়ে—58
পাল্তে মাদার—75
পাসরে—50
পিছাড়ী—78
পিণ্ডারী—40

পীরোত্তর—80
পুষিলাল—75
পূবেন—76
পেছোন—73
পেতি—82
পেতি-কৌআ—82
পেতি-মেকুর—82
পেয়ারা—54
পেয়ালা—54
পের্মাই—56
পেল্লায়—56
পেল্লাদে—56
পোনা—71
পোলো—53
পৌনে—54
পঁউআ—66
পঁড়িত—57
পুঁটী মাছ—64
পুঁতুল—57
পুঁজ—57
পোঁছ—72
পোঁছাই—72
পোঁটা—57
প্যায়রা—54
প্যালা—54
প্রজাহায়—84

ফরাশ—69
ফরাস—69
ফাজলাম,-মি—74
ফুল-ডুঙ্গরী—35
ফুল-ম্-পেড়ে—66
ফাঁস—70

বই—86
বউল—65
বকনা—61
বকা—78
বকাটে—78
বখা—78

বখাটে—78
বছর-ভর—51
বছরের-টা—78
বটে—51
বট্-ঠাকুর—52
বড়-ঠাকুর—52
বড়াল—74
বড়োদাদা—90
বড়্দা—90
বদনাম—82
বদনামী—82
বদভ্যাস—82
বনেলা—76
ব'রো—58
বলদ—53
বলা-টলা—34
বল্লম—69
বষ্টুমী—75
বস্তুতঃ—80
ব'স্-থেকে—52
বহি, বহী—86
বাইচ—77
বাওঁগুলিয়া—66
বাকতা—37
বাগাৎ—84
বাগে—86
বাঘরোল—79
বাঘা-ভাল্কো—54
বাঙন—66
বা'চ—77
বাছুর—54
বাটাল—74
বাটাটা—52
বাট্টে—52
বাড়াও—72
বাড়ি—86
বানান—73
বানানিয়া—73
বানী—59
বাবুআন্—84

বাম্‌নাই—72
বার—89
বারাসে—66
বারাস্তা—58
বালটিকরী—35
বালতো—75
বালদো—75
বালাম্‌চি—77
বালিতুয়া—75
বাসোয়া—56
বাহাউল্লা—58
বাহিচ—77
বাহী—77
বাহুল্য—58
বিকাও—72
বিঘৎ—62
বিছুরে—67
বিরদ, বিরোদ—56
বির্‌হৎ—56
বিল—36
বিল-কেন্দুয়া—37
বিশ—89
বিসরে—67
বুইল—93, 97
বুক—56, 61
বুজুর্গান্‌—84
বুরুল—79
বুলিল—93
বেওরা—65
বেঙ্গ—77
বেঙ্গাচি—77
বেদ্‌ড়া—70
বেন—59
বেনা—54
বেন্নন—57
বেয়ান—59
বেসাত—52, 64, 78
বেসাতি—52, 64, 78
বেহাইন—59
বেহালা—54

বোঝাই—72
বোরো ধান—58
বোল—92, 93
বোল (আমের)—65
বাঁউক—61
বাঁউণ্ডুলে—66
বাঁক—61
বাঁহুক—61
বেঁটে বাঙ্কুরা—66
ব্যাদ্‌ড়া—70
ব্যান—59
ব্যায়লা—54
ব্রহ্মত্তর—80
ব্রহ্মত্রা—80
ব্রহ্মোত্তর—80

ভগমান্‌—66
ভগবান্‌—66
ভাগিনা—52
ভাগ্‌নে—52
ভাগ্যিমানী—66
ভাথী—64
ভাল—53
ভাল-মানুষী—53
ভালা—53
ভালো—53
ভালো মানুষ—53
ভাল্‌—53
ভাল্‌-মান্‌ষি—53
ভাসান—73
ভিজাল, ভেজাল—74
ভিমরুল—79
ভিংরুল—79
ভেক—62
ভেথ—62
ভোগানে—73
ভোর—51

মউনী—73
মউলা, মউলো—75

মওড়া—37
মড়ঞ্চিয়া—77
মড়্‌ঞ্চে—77
মড়্‌ঞ্চে পোয়াতি—77
মতিলাল—75
মদ্দা—82
মদ্দা-গণ্ডার—82
মধ্যস্থ—81
-ময়—80
ময়না—59
ময়রা—55
ময়ান—52, 53
মহড়া—37
মহুড়া—37
মাওয়ালি—75
মাকড়সা—61
মাকসা, মাকোসা—61
মাঝুয়া—90
মাঠাল—74
মাতল—55
মাতোয়ারা—55
মাতোয়ালা—55
মাদী—82
মাদী-হাতী—82
মানুষের দিগকে—83
মানুষের দিগে—83
মান্দারন—72
মায়—69, 87
মারুলি—79
মাস-ভর—51
মিছ্‌-কউনে—72
মিছ্‌-কহনিয়া—72
মিঠাই—73
মিঠেন—76
মিদ্দা—56
মিদ্দে—70
মিড্যা—56, 70
মির্দা—56
মিল-মিলাও—72
মিশাল—74

মিশালি, মিশিলি, মিশেলি—74
মুখ্যতঃ—80
মুচি—67
মুছি—67
মুই—95
মৃধা—56
মেওয়াজাৎ—84
মেওয়াহ—84
মেচতা—78
মেচা—76, 78
মেচাদা—76
মেচ্কা, মেচ্কো—76
মেছতা—78
মেজদা, মেজ্দা—90
মেজো—90
মেজো দাদা—90
মেঝো—90
মেটে—42
মেটে ফিরিঙ্গি—42
মেদি—82
মেদি-শিয়াল—82
মেলানী—73
মেস্তা—78
মৈষাল—75
মোচরমান—70
মোচা—39
মোতিলাল—75
মোহন-ভোগ—61
মৌনী—73
মৌহারী—53
মুঁহি—90

যত—77
যতেক—77
যদ্দিন—52
যাইছে—60
যাই তাই—54
যাং—95
যাচ্ছে—60
যাত—49
যাত্রা—49
যাথেকে—67
যাবে'অথন—91
যাবেয়্যা'ন—91
যিএই—95
যিয়—96
যিয়চ্—96
যিয়ন্—96
যিয়ে—96
যিয়েই—96
যে—91
যেই—95
যেইয়াং—95
যেদ্দাও—52
যেন—93
যোগানে'—73
যাঁহাদের—91

রইদ—67
রউদ্দ—67
রওয়াক—55
রক্—55
রসম্—41
রাগত—71
রাজহাঁস—82
রাত-ভর—51
রিশবৎ—69
রুজু—56
-রুল—79
রে—54
রোয়াক—55
-রোল—79
রাঁধনী—72, 75
র‍্যা—52, 54, 67
র‍্যা-কানা হ'ল্‌ছে—67

লইয়া—103
লক্ষ—89
লড়াইস্থ—81
লতানে'—73
লয়্যা—103
লাখ—89
লাগাও—72
লাঙ্গড়া—70
লাং (ল্যাং) মারা—57
লার্ (root)—102
লোপাট—78
ল্যাঙ্গ ড়া—70

শক্ত—70
শক্তিগড়—35
শদ—55
শ'-বাজার—55
শরম—70
শাইকোট—67
শাপটিকট—67
শার্মোনিয়ম—67
শালিক—61
শালিখ—61
শালুক—61
শিকদার—69
শিখ—62
শিঙ্গাল, শিঙ্গেল—75
শিমুল-ডাঙ্গা—37
শুকুদ্দিতে—52
শেয়ালা—55
শেহালা—55
শোভা-বাজার—55
শাঁখ-টিকর—35
শ্যাওলা—55
শ্যায়লা—55

সওয়ার—40
সওয়ারি—40
সকড়ি, সকড়ী—58
সথ—70
সঙ্—55
সঙ্গে-সঙ্গে—57
সদ্—55
সব—50

সবটুকু(ন)—88
সভ—51
সভান—51
সভানের—51
সভাস্থ—81
সমী—55
সরম—70
সরাই-টিকর—35
সাইঝ্যা—90
সাউঝুআ—90
সাতাসে—58, 66
সাবড়া—78
সাবাড়—78
সাম্বর—41
সাহেব-গা-র—84
সাহেবান্—84
সিকা, সিকি—89
সুআ, সুও—54
সুখ-জাগানিয়া—73
সুতালি,-লী—75
সুক্কল—79
সুরেলা—76
সুহা—54
সুয্যি—49
সে—91
সেজো—90
সেজো দাদা—90
সেজ্‌দা—90
সেঝো—90
সেটা—78
সেহার—84
সো—54
সোপ—65
সোয়াদ—55
সোয়ামী—55
সোথীন—70
সঁকড়ি—58
সঁতে—87
সঁথে—87
সাঁধানো—51
সিঁধ—51
সেঁঝুতি—52
সেঁধানো—51
-স্থ—81

হইছে—60
হ'চ্ছে—60
হনে—87
হাইরে—58
হাজা—36
হাজা নদী—36
হাটুরে—78
হাড়—64
হাড়াই—72
হারাণে—73
হারাইয়া—58
হারিয়ে—58
হালুয়া—69
হিজ্‌ড়া—70
হিন্দু—69
হিমেল—76
হেইরে—58
হাঁটানে বেটা—73
হাঁড়াল—74
হাঁড়িয়াল—74
হাঁড়ীশাল—61
হাঁফানি,-নী—73
হেঁট—50
হেঁড়েল—74
হেঁশেল—61
হোঁড়ল—74
হোঁদল—74

SUPPLEMENTARY VOLUME

I Additions and Corrections (Revised to March 1971)

II Index of Bengali Words in the Supplementary Volume

'The Origin and Development of the Bengali Language' was published in 1926, and it has been printed again by Offset Process in 1970–1971. Certain new 'Additions and Corrections' have now become necessary. In this *Supplementary Volume*, these Additions and Corrections, revised to March 1971, have been printed. These include *all* the 'Additions and Corrections' which appeared in the Original Volume II of the work (pp. 1059–1078) as reprinted, and they are now entirely cancelled—this *Supplementary Volume* gives all the 'Additions and Corrections' for the entire book in Two Volumes as now printed once again. The 'Index of Bengali Words' in the present *Supplementary Volume*, with references to the new pagination for this volume, is a continuation of the original 'Index of Bengali Words' as in Volume II (pp. 1081–1179), and as such this original 'Index' is not cancelled.

SUNITI KUMAR CHATTERJI

May 9, 1971

For Product Safety Concerns and Information please contact our EU
representative GPSR@taylorandfrancis.com
Taylor & Francis Verlag GmbH, Kaufingerstraße 24, 80331 München, Germany

www.ingramcontent.com/pod-product-compliance
Lightning Source LLC
Chambersburg PA
CBHW061418300426
44114CB00015B/1978
* 9 7 8 1 0 3 2 7 7 0 6 8 0 *